CARING ENOUGH TO CONFRONT

CARING ENOUGH to CONFRONT

HOW TO UNDERSTAND AND EXPRESS YOUR DEEPEST FEELINGS TOWARD OTHERS

David Augsburger

Revell
a division of Baker Publishing Group
Grand Rapids, Michigan

Published by Revell
a division of Baker Publishing Group
PO Box 6287, Grand Rapids, MI 49516-6287
www.revellbooks.com

Revell edition published 2014
ISBN 978-0-8007-2844-1

First edition, 1973 (Herald Press)
Second edition, 1981 (Herald Press)
Third edition, 2009 (Regal)

Printed and bound in the UK, July 2016, LH26

The Library of Congress has cataloged the previous edition as follows:
Augsburger, David.
Caring enough to confront / David Augsburger. Rev. ed.
p. cm.
1. Christian life—Mennonite authors. 2. Conflict (Psychology)
BV4501.2.A883 1980
248.4'897—dc 19 80123568

14 15 16 17 18 19 20 7 6 5 4 3 2 1

CONTENTS

PREFACE TO THE THIRD EDITION

How to differ with others: Confront others as you would have them confront you. How to disagree: Speak to others as you would want them to speak to you. How to offer help: Respect the other's right to refuse your help as you would like to be able to refuse his or hers. All of these are forms of caring; each of these reveals and offers the secret of effective confronting that is necessary to constructive relating.

"Creative living is care-fronting in conflict." These words that introduced the preface to this manuscript in the spring of 1973 are, more than a quarter-century later, even more true. The opportunity to totally rewrite, update and improve this book on conflict is a testimony that it is even more needed, more appropriate to a world of contrasts in goals and differences in relationships.

When your thrust as a person—your hopes, dreams, wants, needs, drives for meaning, significance, vitality—runs counter to my thrust, there may be conflict. To sacrifice your thrust is to be untrue to the push and pull of life, of hope, of God at work within you. To negate my own thrust is to refuse to be fully open to the presence and work of God within my life. Integrating your needs and wants with my needs and wants in our joint effort toward creating Christian community is effective living.

It is not conflict that needs to concern us, but how the conflicts are handled. The frontal impact of our coming together can be creative, strengthening and growth producing. This concern for a balanced wholeness of personal integrity and sensitivity to persons runs throughout these essays on care-fronting as a creative way of uniting care, candor and confrontation in life relationships.

The teachers, colleagues and friends who taught me to appreciate conflict and speeded my slowness to learn are many:

Frank Kimper, Howard J. Clinebell, Jr., Jan and Myron Chartier, H. Newton Maloney, Speed Leas, Marcus Smucker, Alvin Dueck, Mohammed Abu Nimer, Glen Stassen, as well as hundreds of students who question, confront and keep asking their teacher to be edgy and growing.

"You wrote a book called *Caring Enough to Confront*," a man from an audience once asked. "What else have you written that doesn't work?" The audience laughed appreciatively. We all can tell stories of painful failures in our conflicts and confrontations as well as hopeful moments of success when the caring is believed and the confrontation is received with the respect in which it is given, and we move toward new understanding. This is a continuation of such stories of hope.

I love you.

If I love you,
I must tell you the truth.

If I tell you the truth

Will you hear my love?
Will you hear love in my truth?

I want your love.

I want your truth.

Love me enough
to tell me the truth.

"Finish, then, with lying and let each . . .
tell his neighbor the truth,
for we are all parts of the same body."

St. Paul, Letter to the Ephesians (4:25, *Phillips*)

I

CARE-FRONTING:

A Creative Way Through Conflict

"Caring." Obviously a good word.

"Confronting"? Frequently a bad word.

Both are highly important relational words. Put together they provide the unique combination of love and truth that is necessary for building effective human relationships.

The more common practice is to keep these two distinct and separate.

"There is a time for caring. There is a time for confronting."

"Care when caring is called for, confront when confrontation is required."

"Each in its own place, each in its own right time."

Caring dare not be contaminated by any mixture of confrontation. And confronting must not be diluted by any admixture of caring. Each weakens the other. To confront powerfully, lay care aside. To care genuinely, candor and confrontation must be forgotten, for the moment at least.

"When someone matters to me—really matters, I do not dare to disagree: to differ is to disrespect; I cannot confront, because hurting another is the very last thing I want."

"When I'm angry, I confront. To talk of caring at a moment like that would be false. I speak the truth as I see it and let the chips fly from my shoulder to fall where they may."

A third word: "Care-fronting." A good word.

Care-fronting is offering genuine caring that lifts, supports and encourages the other. (To care is to bid another to grow, to welcome, invite and support growth in another.)

Care-fronting is being upfront with important facts that can call out new awareness, insight and understanding. (To confront effectively is to offer the maximum of useful information with the minimum of threat and stress.)

Care-fronting is loving and level conversation. It unites the love one has for the other with the honest truth that I am able to see about the two of us. Care-fronting unifies concern for relationship with concerns for goals—my goals, your goals, our goals. So one can have something to stand for (goals) as well as someone to stand with (relationship) without sacrificing one for the other or collapsing one into another. This allows each of us to be genuinely loving without giving away one's power to think, choose and act. In such honesty, one can love powerfully and be powerfully loving. These are not contradictory. They are complementary. (The opposite is to express powerless love until anger erupts in loveless power—to yield in pseudo-love until one overloads to the breaking point and then explode with demands heated to the boiling point.)

"That was a tasteless thing to do, just like your mother . . ." your husband mutters over dinner. You swallow twice at food gone flat, freeze into angry silence, get up from the table. (He shows no surprise at this familiar routine. You fumble a response to one of the kids, his critical words cut to the quick and you retreat to lick the wound.)

You see in the shrug of his shoulders that he knows your next move—flight to the bedroom, an evening and night of cold, withdrawn anger. When you feel rejected, you reject. (So? He cuts you off, and off you go to sulk.)

"What have I ever gained by running?" you ask yourself. "The longer I brood, the more I hurt. I know what I need to do.

Talk, not walk—tell him what I'm feeling." (Would you dare to go back, to say what you feel, what you need, what you want?)

"Perhaps the time is now," you decide. You slow the feelings that press to rush out. You weigh and then say what really matters to you, what is your truth.

"When you criticize me like that, I feel rejected. I hurt. I usually run. But what I really want is to tear down the prickly hedge between us and to be able to feel close to you again. And to do that, I need—I want—in fact, I demand that you respect me as me. I am not my mother. I am who I am." He's silent. He nods in surprise. He's not used to hearing feelings and needs described so clearly. He's seldom heard you say what you really want.

(Memo to self: When cut by sharp words, silent withdrawal is self-defeating. Explosive counterattack is self-destructive. What is needed is a clear, nondefensive statement of what I feel, need, want. If I confront with what I really want, I am caring enough about our getting together, to risk.)

Care-fronting is, arguably, the most valuable secret for reforming conflicts. To care and to be clear at the same time is mature relating; to be truly for the other and to stand for what you value when with the other, without sacrificing either, is not just to be adept at interpersonal communication; it is what it means to be adult. The twin abilities of (1) concern for the other and (2) commitment to one's freely chosen goals do not need to be sacrificed, compromised or conflicted. They can both be sought in harmony and healthful assertiveness.

Care-fronting has a unique view of conflict. It sees conflict as natural, normal, neutral and sometimes even delightful. It recognizes that conflict can turn into painful or disastrous ends, but it doesn't need to. Conflict of itself is neither good nor bad, right nor wrong. Conflict simply is. How we view, approach and work through our differences does—to a large extent—determine our whole life pattern.

None of the four most common views about conflict—that it is inevitable and hopeless, that it is dangerous and frightening, that it is a simple issue of right-over-wrong, that it calls for constant compromise—none of these seeks to transform the problem situation. They each and all seek to avoid, escape, fix, suppress or force a resolution.

If I, for example, view conflict as *a given,* as *a fixed matter of fate*, explaining, "We just can't get along—we're incompatible—we'll never understand each other—that's all there is to it," then my life pattern would be one of *avoiding* threat, *withdrawing* and going my own isolated, escapist, well-armored way. "Confronting is useless, caring is hopeless, we are helpless, it is best to flee."

If I, as conflict prone, view conflict as *an inevitable issue* of right and wrong, "I owe it to you to save you from yourself; to me to be right; to God to defend His (our) truth and show others their error," then my life will uphold and maintain the right even if it requires *pressuring, forcing* and, above all, *winning.* "Conflict is a matter of who, not what is right. I happen to be right (of course) and you wrong (no offense), so yield."

If I, as conflict shy, see conflict as *crushing,* as *threatening,* as *disastrous,* warning myself, "If we clash, I'll be judged—be rejected—our friendship will fall through," then my life pattern would be acting nice guy or gal, quickly yielding and *accommodating* to keep things comfortable. "Confronting is dangerous; caring is giving in; it is best to fold."

If I, as a civil person, see conflict as *a mutual difference* to be resolved by meeting each other halfway, "I'll come part way, you come part way. Let's cooperate, compromise or put our heads together in some joint way," then my life pattern will be a *compromising,* meet-me-in-the-middle style of one-for-me-and-one-for-you cooperation. "Conflict is best resolved by vote. Civilization is built upon compromise. Let's start from the middle."

There is a fifth view: I can come to see conflict as *natural, neutral, normal.* I may then be able to see the difficulties we experience as tensions in relationships and honest differences in perspective that can be worked through in *collaboration* created by each caring about the other and each confronting the other with truthfulness and neighbor love. "Conflict is the opportunity to become co-creators of a joint solution—let's risk open trust, honest self-disclosure and frank confrontation."

Each of these five positions, if they are the dominant styles of facing conflict, will shape a person's basic life pattern. A combination of two, three or four of the five will often characterize the conflict repertoire of most adults in your life.

If you utilize these five conflict attitudes and behaviors in the order listed above (avoid, coerce, yield, compromise, then create a joint outcome), you are frequently frustrated, misunderstood, alienated or often painfully confused about yourself and others. This is a frequent sequence for conflict-avoidant, conflict-defensive or conflict-shy persons. There is a time and a place for each of the five styles, but to make avoidance the main organizing response, or to follow yielding or forcing as the predominant way of dealing with differences is rarely useful or effective.

If your preferences of these perspectives on conflict are in reverse order (that is, to seek to find a creative collaborative solution first, and as a backup seek a compromise to build on in seeking to construct a mutually satisfactory solution; and only then, if necessary, yield to strengthen relationship, and delay taking a stubborn position or withdrawing until the very end), then you may be already chuckling and feeling good about the skills that you either inherited or learned for resolving conflict. Whatever your present skill set, new skills can be learned. You'll add at least one by the end of this chapter.

"He's stealing me blind," you say, numb with anger. "More than $300 must have come in across the counter today, and his cash register ticket shows $175.

"Of all the stupid blunders, going into a partnership with my brother-in-law has got to be the all-time winner," you say. Opening your pharmacy together had seemed so right. But in the first nine months you've barely turned a profit.

"The rat. He's been pocketing the cash, ringing up no-sales, or avoiding the register altogether." Whatever the system, he's picking you clean.

"I'll get him. I'll fix his wagon good, the embezzler." Oh, but you can't. It'll hurt your sister more than him, and she's just pulling away from a long depression.

"I'll shut up and get out. He can buy my half and have the whole thing—debt, mortgage and all—right in his inadequate lap." Not so easy. Your home was mortgaged too for the operating capital. You're in all the way. To get out, you'll have to let him know you know.

"I'll give in and just sit on it for the time being. I'll wait for the auditor to catch it, or for him to hang himself by getting even greedier. (Maybe if I give him a bonus, or commend him more for his work it will make him feel unbearably guilty.)

"I'll go halfway, I'll go along with him for a while, not say a thing, just stick so close he'll have to play fair." But breathing down his neck as you peer over his shoulder is a temporary compromise solution. You can't be there all the time.

"I've got to gather my facts, find the best time, let him know that his future matters to me as well as my own, and then confront him with the goods. There's no other way out of the mess. But can I do it?"

(Memo to self: If I act to win by insuring that he loses—we both lose in the end; if I avoid, put it off or look the other way, we both lose even more. I must find a way for us to meet, talk, face reality and seek a just outcome that has integrity and logical consequences but does not seek to annihilate or destroy the other.)

The five options: (1) I'll get him; (2) I'll get out; (3) I'll give in; (4) I'll meet halfway; or (5) I care enough to confront.

Collaborate and recreate the relationship are the basic alternatives open in most conflict situations.

1. *"I'll get him"* is the I-win-you-lose-because-I'm-right-you're-wrong position in conflict. From this viewpoint, the attitude toward conflict is that the issues are all quite clear—and simple. Someone is right—totally right, and someone is wrong—completely wrong. Fortunately, I'm right (as usual) and you're wrong. It's my duty to put you right. This "win-lose" stance relies on the use of power and utilizes little or no love. Goal is valued above relationship. "My way is the only way," the person feels. In the Conflict Behavior Survey (see Appendix 1), this approach is called **"My way—win/lose."** There are times when "My-way" may be useful—when time is very short, the task is extremely crucial—like a rescue effort in an emergency—or someone is being taken advantage of and intervention is necessary, like reporting child abuse or intervening in spousal abuse. One may act decisively, but recognize that later the action will need to be reviewed.

2. *"I'll get out"* is the I'm-uncomfortable-so-I'll-withdraw stance toward conflict. The viewpoint here is that conflicts are hopeless, people cannot be changed; we either overlook them or withdraw. Conflicts are to be avoided at all costs. When they threaten, get out of their way. Withdrawal has its advantages if instant safety is the all-important thing. But it is a way out of conflict, not a way through. And a way out is no way at all.

In this "lose-lose" stance, everyone loses. There is no risk of power, no trusting love. "Show me to the nearest exit," the person requests over the shoulder. In the Conflict Behavior Survey it is called, **"No way—avoid."** However, it should be recognized that situations requiring withdrawal do arise, such as when you have no power, or you need to count to ten to cool off, or the damage that would be inflicted by any confrontation is too great for a very sensitive person to deal with, or often when the issue is trivial and not worth addressing.

3. *"I'll give in"* is the I'll-yield-to-be-nice-since-I-need-your-friendship approach. This perspective on conflict says that differences are disastrous. If such issues come out into the open, anything could happen. Anything negative, evil or destructive, that is. It's far better to be nice, to submit, to go along with the other's demands and stay friends.

Yielding to keep contact will serve you well in many situations. But as a rule of life, it falls short. You become a doormat. A nice guy or gal. Frustrated, yet smiling. The more tense and tight on the inside, the more generous and submissive on the outside. In the Conflict Behavior Survey it is called, **"Thy way—yield."** Yielding is sometimes the path of wisdom. If you suspect that you could be wrong, or you need to build credit on this issue to use on another in the future that matters much more, or when harmony is more important than the particular difference, or even when you decide that it is better for the other to learn by risking, choosing, and even by learning from a mistake.

4. *"I'll meet you halfway"* is the I-have-only-half-the-truth-and-I-need-your-half position. The attitude is one of creative compromise. Conflict is natural, and everyone should be willing to come partway in an attempt to resolve things. A willingness to give a little will lead to a working solution that is satisfactory to everyone.

Compromise is a gift to human relationships. We move forward on the basis of thoughtful, careful consensus and compromise in most decisions in conflict. But it calls for at least a partial sacrifice of deeply held views and goals that may cost all of us the loss of the best to reach the good of agreement. To reach compromise, often each side gives up the portion of their position that they valued most and keeps that part that was of less interest or concern. So both sides feel depleted, disillusioned, dissatisfied with the outcome.

When compromise is our automatic first choice, we run the risk that my half of the truth added to your half may not give us the "truth, the whole truth and nothing but the truth." We may have two half-truths. Or the combination may produce a whole untruth. Only when we care enough to tussle with truth can we test, retest, refine and perhaps find more of it through our working at it seriously. In the Conflict Behavior Survey, this position is called **"Our way—fifty/fifty."** This option is sometimes the better choice when the goals are only moderately important, so relinquishing half is quite acceptable; when time is a factor and you need to reach a decision immediately; or when a temporary settlement is satisfactory and will work until a later review can revise it.

5. *"I care enough to confront, care enough to recreate the relationship"* is the position that persists in pursuing an outcome with the twin goals of I-want-relationship-and-I-also-want-honesty-and-integrity. Conflict is viewed as neutral (neither good nor bad) and natural (neither to be avoided nor short-circuited). Working through differences by giving clear messages of "I care" and "I want," which both care and confront, is most helpful.

This is interpersonal communication that is not easily discouraged or sidetracked. It seeks to stay connected while refusing to give up on the goals. It is caring—I want to stay in respectful relationship with you, *and* confronting—I want you to know where I stand and what I'm feeling, needing, valuing and wanting. In Conflict Behavior Survey terms, it is called **"Third way—joint creativity."** This is the option we hope to create in order to take both sets of concern and vision seriously, since it strengthens both the commitment to the goal and to the relationship. It draws upon and deepens the simple humanness of both sides and of the network of relationships that surrounds them in their work together.

CARING	CONFRONTING
I care about you and about our relationship.	I feel deeply about the issues and interests at stake.
I want to hear your view.	I want to clearly express mine.
I want to fully respect your insights.	I want authentic respect for mine.
I trust you to be able to handle my honest feelings.	I want you to trust me with yours, knowing I can handle them fairly.
I promise to stay with the discussion until we've reached an understanding.	I want you to keep working with me until we've reached a new understanding.
I will not pressure, manipulate, or distort the differences.	I want your unpressured, clear, undistorted view of our differences.
I give you my loving, honest respect.	I want your caring-confronting response.

To visualize the interrelationship of caring and confronting, of love and power, of concern about relationships and concern for goals, the diagram (figure 1) places these two values on the scale of intensity measured from one to nine. This offers four quadrants and a center point of cooperation/compromise.

The "I-leave-I-lose" quadrant has little commitment to being either assertive or affirmative (thus measured on the one-to-nine scales, it is called a 1/1 stance of **"No way—avoidance"**).

The "I-yield-to-win-acceptance" quadrant shows high commitment to maintaining or deepening relationships of approval but little to expressing a personal commitment to any threaten-

FIGURE 1

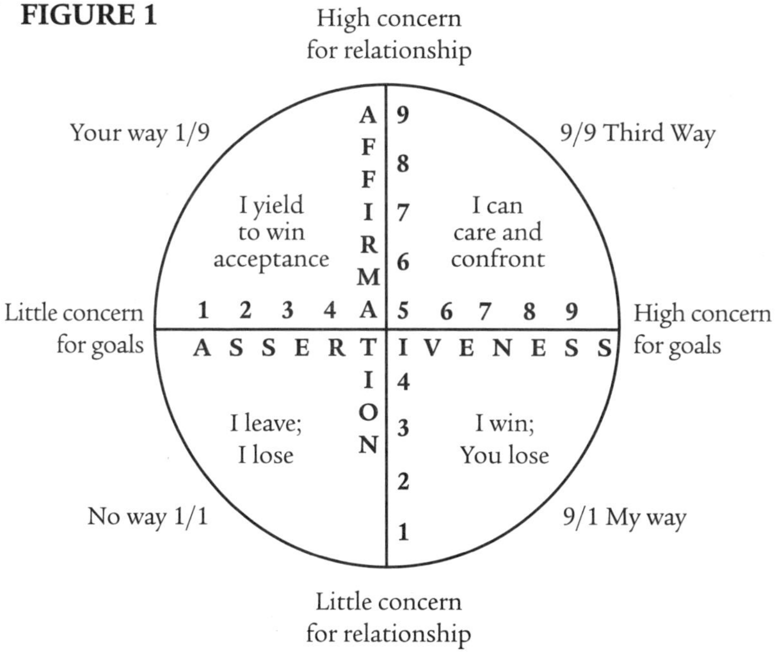

ing goal (thus it is high on affirmation, but is unassertive in a 1/9 stance of **"Your way—yield"**).

The "I-win-you-lose" quadrant is all assertiveness, and often pure aggressiveness with little affirmation of the personal elements that prize relationships (thus 9/1, **"My way—force"**).

The center of the diagram is the cooperative or compromising "Let's-each-come-halfway, meet-me-in-the-middle" stance (thus 5/5, **"Our way—fifty/fifty"**).

The "I-will-care-and-confront" quadrant is the caring and confronting stance that places high value on both personal relationships and personal goals by seeking to create mutual relationships that work out joint and satisfactory solutions (thus 9/9, **"Third way—joint creativity"**).

Each of these responses has its place in life. Each style of behavior has its appropriate time, situation and use.

The most effective usages are to begin insistently by (1) caring and confronting. If this is not effective in calling out a joint effort at reaching a mutually satisfactory solution, then (2) movement to a cooperative-compromise stance is well advised. This is hopefully a temporary solution that will open the opportunity to move toward enhanced caring and increased candor. If this fails, (3) it is wise to move toward a yield-to-maintain-relationship stance. Not as an end state, but as an intermediate commitment to build relationship so that more effective conversations and negotiations may follow. Only if this is rejected is it wise to move to (4) a win-lose stance of affirming goals even at the cost of sacrificing relationships. The hope, even in taking this assertive stance, is that one will be able to clarify the situation sufficiently to return to an equally affirmative and assertive relationship. If all of these prove ineffective, last choice (5) is a leave-and-lose move of withdrawal. Regretfully, one respects the other's right to refuse, reject or withdraw for a period of separate growth and discovery. The conflict is alleviated by this; but the story has not reached the end.

Of the five options in conflict situations—(1) I win–you lose; (2) I want out, I'll withdraw; (3) I'll give in for good relations; (4) I'll meet you halfway; (5) I can care and confront—the last is the most effective, the most truly loving, the most growth-promoting for human relationships. But often it will not be the starting point, but the long-term goal.

When a person comes on strong with "I win–you lose," it may be appropriate to respond with an "I'll give in for good relations" until the immediate storm is past. Then you can move back to an "I can care and confront" discussion.

When another responds immediately with an "I want out–I withdraw" attitude, choosing to work toward a compromise or a temporary focus on the relationship can be appropriate for the moment to affirm your deep interest in continuing friendship. But moving back to care-confront openness as soon as possible is important to you both.

Rigid fixation in any one style or exaggerated dependence on any one behavior will seldom be effective. The ability to respond in varied ways, and the flexibility to match one's response to the shape a conflict is taking, are crucial skills to be added to year by year.-

The Conflict Behavior Survey in Appendix 1 provides a testing instrument that will give a useful reading on your preference for (1) a particular way of responding, (2) the pattern of preferences as you move from one style to another, and (3) the comparison of which conflict behaviors are most developed and employed versus those that are less practiced and seldom used. Follow the instructions on how to take the survey several times while thinking of different relationships so that you can contrast and compare how you respond in differing situations.

"Why did you stay out with the car last night when we had agreed it would be back—did you forget I'd be needing it?" your husband says to your son—actually, to your son's indifferent back. He shrugs his shoulders in reply.

"What were you thinking?"

"Man, it was a track meet," your son replies. "It wasn't over until it was over."

"Don't you know that a promise is a promise?" the dad asks.

The boy is ignoring his win-lose questioning. To answer is to walk into a bear trap. If he answers, his dad will point out that his reason was stupid. It's like an unending cycle, fight and flight, move and countermove, talking past each other.

"I want to know why you deliberately defy me. Is it just to spite me?" your husband is asking.

"Is there no end to their fights?" you wonder.

(Memo to self: Maybe they could use a referee who could get them to agree to some simple ground rules that would enable them to fight more fairly. Not you, most likely. Use your power to get them to seek a good trainer.)

When conflicts over different issues all seem to end the same way, something is going wrong. Or when conflict recurs repeatedly over the same issue, something deeper than that issue is causing the problem. Rigid patterns are triumphing over right relationships; frozen attitudes about conflict are blocking communication and collaboration. Getting the perspective of a third party can be of great help in opening one's style of handling stress or learning new ways to work at differences.

For example, conflict training can help a person, a couple or a family incorporate a new set of guidelines for cleaning up fights and making them more mutually beneficial, such as: the person who has a complaint should make the first move to schedule a discussion session; fight only at an agreed upon time and place; one complaint to a session; no trapping questions, just clear statements. Give honest, clean "beefs" (sharply pointed complaints or issues) like, "The behavior you do is . . ."; "When you do it, I feel . . ."; "What I really want is . . ." The receiver repeats the beef to show that it was heard and replies with a differing perspective. The sender takes this into consideration in the request, "What I really want is . . ." The responder answers with a "need time to think about it," gives a clear yes or no, makes a compromise offer, or the two can seek a third way that satisfies the issues and interests on both sides. So that both get heard, both move toward the other and both find new options.

There are many effective strategies for working through to agreement. What matters is the balance of concern for the relationship and concern for issues—or to put it another way, the commitment to the welfare of all involved balanced with appropriate concern for the issues and interests that are at stake. If care for the neighbor and clarity in confrontation on the issues are not split—one is not sacrificed to gain the other, people feel like their truth has been heard and honored—people feel respected and cared for in relationship.

As a model of the ability to respond genuinely and appropriately with both love and power in balance, two millennia of Christians have looked to the confrontive, caring and creative relationships modeled in the Gospel stories of the life of Jesus of Nazareth. Every teacher, counselor or mediator envisions a model of optimum human maturity and projects a person who characterizes this high level of functioning. Inevitably, Christ's followers look to Him for such a model of maturity. However, all combined in the four Gospel stories, we have only six hours of His teaching and can account for only 50 of the 1,000 days of his public ministry.

Psychological analysis of Jesus is not appropriate nor is it possible; yet the imitation of Christ remains as the greatest challenge in human history. It is the inevitable impact of His surprising and revolutionary example. We need not use the stories of His life to attach moral values to particular conflict behaviors, or to bless any particular theory or set of behavioral practices. We can, however, profit from examining His responses to various situations as examples of ways to respond to conflict or confrontation. If we dare to use the language of conflict styles as a way of picturing His human relationships, we will be immediately struck by His willingness to use all five of the human conflict responses we have been studying in this chapter in His various dealings with significant people in His life; and we will note the consistency of His actions with His stated goals of redemptive compassion.

When the less-than-friendly hometown people of Nazareth rejected His message of confronting love, He chose to withdraw (see Luke 4:14-30). He cut off conversation and debate with the Pharisees when the point of clear rejection had arrived (see John 11:45-57). When Pilate dismissed His words with the rhetorical question "What is truth?" He withdrew into silence and ended the conversation.

Jesus was also free to act in an "I win-you lose" manner when this was the way to clearest understanding. He confronted the hucksters and hustlers in the Temple on win–lose terms (see Mark 11:11-19). Or read His clear statements to the religious leaders in Matthew 23, given after they had willed and arranged for His death.

At His arrest, during His interrogation, throughout His trial, in His unjust beating, and even through His execution, Jesus chose to absorb the anger of others, submit to unjust suffering, and speak back the word of forgiveness, grace and acceptance.

There are no examples of such integrity in conflict like His; He cared—and confronted—with exemplary consistence, courage and clarity. No model offers the distinctive balance between care for persons and concern for virtues than did Jesus.

To the would-be executioners of an accused adulteress, Jesus listened, waiting to hear their persistent questioning, to record all charges in the dust. *The active behavior of caring.* Then He said, "Let the one among you who has never sinned throw the first stone at her." *An unparalleled accuracy in confrontation.*

To the woman, He said, " 'Where are they all—did no one condemn you?' . . . 'No one, sir,' 'Neither do I condemn you.' " *Warm, understanding care.* "Go away now and do not sin again." *Clear, unmistakable confrontation* (John 8:7,10-11, *Phillips*).

To the rich, vain, conceited young ruler, Jesus listened, responded clearly, then looked at him and loved him. Then Jesus confronted. "Go, sell all, give to the poor; and come follow me" (see Mark 10:17-31). What could be more clear?

To Nicodemus (see John 3), to the outcast minority-group woman at the public watering place (see John 4), to the mayor of Capernaum whose son is at the point of death (see John 4), Jesus cared and confronted. He spoke truth in love. He was truth. He was love.

In his letter to Christians at Ephesus, Paul described the nature of Christian maturity as modeled in Jesus' own integration of truth and love:

> So shall we all at last attain to the unity inherent in our faith and our knowledge of the Son of God—to mature manhood, measured by nothing less than the full stature of Christ. . . . Let us speak the truth in love; so shall we fully grow up into Christ (Eph. 4:13,15, *NEB*).

John summarized the presence of God in Jesus with these same words.

> So the Word became flesh; he came to dwell among us, and we saw his glory, . . . full of grace and truth (John 1:14, *NEB*).

Truth with love brings healing. Truth told in love enables us to grow. Truth in love produces change. Truth and love are the two necessary ingredients for any relationship with integrity: love—because all positive relationships begin with friendship, appreciation, respect; and truth—because no relationship of trust can long grow from dishonesty, deceit, betrayal; it springs up from the solid stuff of integrity.

The two arms of genuine relationship are: truth reaches out to touch truth; love embraces love. The authenticity, honesty and transparency of truthfulness build trusting relationship; the positive regard of warmth that is not possessive offers affirmation. These are the two movements of relational integrity. I grow most rapidly when supported with the arm of loving respect, with sufficient security to uphold me through any confrontation from the arm of clear honesty. Confronting and caring stimulate growth.

"Confrontation plus caring brings growth just as judgment plus grace brings salvation," Howard Clinebell, Jr., one of the leading pastoral counselors, would say in theological discussion of supporting persons as they are making choices and reporting the reality and consequences of good and bad choices.

This is how, theologically, we speak of the way in which God relates to us. Judgment inseparable from grace, grace undiminished by judgment; together these lead to salvation. God's judgment—radical honesty about truth—confronts us with the demands of disciplined maturity. God's grace—undeserved love—reaches out to accept and affirm us at the point we know ourselves to be unacceptable. If God dealt us only judgment, who could stand? If God reached out to us only in love, it would be a cheap grace without integrity, mere divine permissiveness.

Perhaps we, too, in our efforts to live more justly, can embody grace and truth in difficult circumstances and settings? Perhaps this is our calling to live out such integrity. Is not this, in the last account, the way to maturity?

FOR FURTHER EXPERIENCE

1. Do a mental rehearsal of both caring and confronting in conflicts you experienced today or anticipate tomorrow. Place the other person in a chair in front of you and hold out your left hand, saying, "I do care, I want to respect you, I want your respect." Alternate by reaching out with the right hand to say, "But I want you to know how I feel. I want to tell you where I am. I have this goal in our relationship." Work both sides of yourself. Become aware of which is more difficult. In which are you least practiced? Stay with it until feelings of caring and statements of goal both become clear.

2. Check back through your relationships of the past week. Fill in appropriate situations.

   (1) "My way." I win–you lose stance.

   (2) "No way." I want out–I withdraw attitude.

   (3) "Thy way." I'll give in for good relations.

   (4) "Our way." I'll meet you halfway.

   (5) "Third way." I can care and confront.

Which was effective? Which was most comfortable? Which was used most frequently? Which do you want to use more often?

I want to hear you,
see what you see,
feel what you feel,
think through your thoughts.

So I will make room for you,
Clear away my valuations,
Place my feelings on hold,
Let my experience be only the frame
So your world becomes the picture.
I want to be heard.
I long to be understood,
I have a need to be known.
Listen to me as I listen to you.
So I will speak simply
with clear word windows
that let you see
all the way in
to where I live
laugh and cry.

"Knowing this, then, dear brothers, let every man
be quick to listen but slow to use his tongue,
and slow to lose his temper."

Letter of St. James (1:19, *Phillips*).

2

TRUTHING:

A Simplified Speech Style

A relationship is only as strong as its communication is clear.

Good relationship is two-way communication.

When one side of the conversation is deeply troubled, the relationship is stressed; when one side is lost, the relationship is dying.

To the degree that equal responsiveness is lost, to that extent the relationship ceases to exist.

To love another is to invite, support and protect that person's equal right to hear and be heard.

To love is to listen; to be loved is to be fully heard.

Love is first the action of the eyes attending, the ears attuning and then the soul connecting.

When I *listen:*

I want to hear you—to hear deeply, to hear openly. To attend to what is said, how it is said, what feeling is conveyed, and what is wanted. I want to hear you with the inner ear that is attuned to the feelings, the joys, the hurts, the angers, the demands of another.

I want to hear *you,* by going beyond just hearing myself interpreting you. I am aware of two strong tendencies: (1) to "read in" my interpretations as I listen and miss what you are wanting to tell me; and (2) to "read out" and totally miss what I don't want to hear from you because it threatens, confronts, rejects, ignores me and my viewpoint.

I want to hear you accurately, so I'll need to check out what I hear at crucial points to be as certain as possible that my meanings match your meanings. I get an inkling of what your meanings are from your words, your tone of voice, your face, your gestures, your body movements. But it is only an inkling. I must check it out at times by replaying what I heard for your approval, until you agree that you have been heard.

I want to hear deeply, clearly, accurately enough that I am able—to some real extent—to feel what you feel, hurt where you hurt and want for you the freedom to be all that you are becoming.

When I *speak:*

I want to speak simply—to say what I mean in the clearest, shortest, frankest words I know. I want to reach out with my meanings to meet your meanings. (Communication is a meeting of meaning.) Knowing that meanings are in people, not in words, I want to be as clear and open about my meanings as I can. (Words don't mean. People mean.)

I want to speak personally. Since I can speak only from my experience, I want to say, "I think . . . ," "I feel . . . ," "I want . . . ," instead of "People think . . ." or "You get the feeling . . ." To declare my personal feelings and convictions calls for courage. There is no risk in saying, "Most people," "it seems," "sometimes feel," "to some extent." I will risk; I will reveal my true self; I will be increasingly vulnerable to you by respecting your perceptions equally with my own.

I want to speak for myself, not for others. I will not say, "We think . . ." "they say . . ." "people feel . . ." or "it's often said . . ." I have no right to use other voices instead of my own.

I will not try to speak for you. I will not say, "I think you think I think . . ." I will not try to second-guess your feelings, thoughts, attitudes. I do not care for mind reading or mind readers. I want to listen as you speak to me, and respond.

I want to speak honestly. Truthing is trusting others with my actual feelings and viewpoints. Avoiding honest statements of real feelings and viewpoints is often considered kindness, thoughtfulness or generosity. More often it is the most cruel thing I can do to others. It is benevolent lying. Selective honesty is not honesty at all. I find myself using it (1) to avoid real relationships with others when I'm too rushed or bushed to give them my time; (2) to avoid clear confrontation with others; (3) to manipulate situations or facts to protect myself or others. I don't like such defense systems, no matter what sort of safety they promise. I want to be truthful in all situations. I want to pay others the compliment of believing they too value honesty and can handle honest feelings. I want to put out what I feel, where I am, how I think.

I want to speak directly. I do not want to talk about people when it is possible to talk to them. Whatever I have to say to you, I want you to hear first from me.

When we *conflict:*

I want conflict to call out the best in myself and others. I want to negotiate differences with others in clear, respectful, truthful ways of hearing, speaking and acting. I want both the truth as I see it and respect for the other to be clear in my responses—verbal and nonverbal.

When situations of conflict become difficult, I want to first listen attentively, openly, respectfully and in a way that validates the other's right to a different perspective, different values, different interests and goals. When it is appropriate for me to speak, I want to do so clearly, honestly, personally, directly and in simple statements. This provides the greatest impact with the least confusion or distortion. I may or may not be able to break through the walls blocking our mutual understanding, but I can express both love and truth best by refusing to get caught in the many communication traps, potholes, detours and dead-ends such as the "whys" and the "it's your faults" and the "you must change first" strategies.

I want to love truthfulness in our relationship because only then can I truly love you. In speaking truthfully, I welcome you to the sacred room in my soul where the most important truths about my life are kept. The truths that nourish trust relationships are shared only in authentic self-disclosure. "All truth is self-disclosure," a major philosophic premise of contemporary thought affirms as its starting point. The truth that is revealed in self-disclosure has many aspects: owning what is actual, recognizing what is given within us as potential, affirming what is possible. Such truth sharing opens itself to another—vulnerably yet powerfully. Expressing such truth in trust is a two-way street, with a two-way traffic of honesty. Trust, by its very nature, aims at interpersonal truth. Trusting another with the truth about me is the only authentic way of inviting the other to share the truth of his or her experience. Trusting follows truthing; truthing increases trusting.

"It's okay, honey, no problem," you say to your husband on the phone. It's the fourth night in a row he's chosen to work late and called you with last-minute apologies. It's not really okay with you, even though you keep saying it is. But that's always been your style. Be agreeable, give in, say everything's okay, bottle feelings until finally you explode over some stupidly simple thing and say things you regret as soon as you hear them.

"I've got to start dealing with things as they come up, not just postpone my feelings and let them simmer," you say. "Like that phone call right now. I could have said, 'No, it's not okay. I have special things planned. You've been out the last three nights. I want to be with you tonight.' I could have said it with words that are straight and simple." What stops you from leveling? You stop yourself.

"It's not too late," you tell yourself. "I can still ring him back." You pick up the phone and begin dialing. I'll say, "I want to be with you tonight. Try to change things. Come home on time."

(Memo to self: Keep short books with feelings. Stay up-to-date. Find ways of reporting feelings as or soon after they occur. To care-front, experiment in pairing what is felt ***and*** *what is wanted. "I do care about you* ***and*** *I want to be close. I am lonely and frustrated by our schedules* ***and*** *I want more time together.")*

John Powell, in his wonderful book *Why Am I Afraid to Tell You Who I Am?* writes this description of healthy communication as the actual living stuff that makes up this thing we call human relationship:

> It is certain that a relationship will be only as good as its communication. If you and I can honestly tell each other who we are, that is, what we think, judge, feel, value, love, honor and esteem, hate, fear, desire, hope for, believe in and are committed to, then and then only can each of us grow. Then and then alone can each be what one really is, say what one really thinks, tell what one really feels, express what one really loves. This is the real meaning of authenticity as a person: that my exterior truly reflects my interior. It means I can be honest in the communication of my person to others. And this I cannot do unless you help me. Unless you help me, I cannot grow or be happy or really come alive.
>
> I have to be free and able to say my thoughts to you—to tell you about my judgments and values, to expose to you my fears and frustrations, to admit to you my failures and shames, to share my triumphs—before I can really be sure what it is that I am and can become. I must be able to tell you who I am before I can know

> who I am. And I must know who I am before I can act truly, that is, in accordance with my true self.[1]

"It's been months since we really talked," you say in pained realization. "We've grown so far apart. He has his life; I have mine. Once it was a marriage. Now we see each other daily but do not meet. We each pursue our work. We exhaust all our energy in the job. There's not even the old noise of conflict."

"We need new cue cards, or to reshuffle the old deck. If I had the courage to open things tonight—if I would risk asking for one thing I want, or better, ask about his needs—do I know what he needs or wants? Then perhaps we could hear each other without complaint or request something new without blame?"

Healthy communication—*being* the truth with each other—is made up of the give and take of sending and receiving clear messages. The two basic rules are embarrassingly simple: (1) To communicate a message, make a statement; (2) to ask for a message, use a question. Could anything be more obvious? Not so fast. Simplicity in speech is to *state what should be stated, ask what needs to be asked and refuse to confuse the two.* When questions are used as concealed ways to make statements, or statements are made as concealed questions, confusion results. In healthy communication, there is a strong preference for statements, a wise caution in using questions. Why are questions so suspect? Because they are the most easily distorted form of speech, the most often co-opted and corrupted part of language.

Some questions are simple requests for clarification or for further information and they are highly useful. These are often called open-ended questions because they seek information without trying to predict or control the answer. Closed questions have one obvious response. Often they are a strategy for directing, dominating or controlling the other. When used as hit-and-run questions, they are ways of making comments, criticisms or attacks while avoiding the full responsibility for what is said. They are double-talk ways of giving multilevel messages that leave the listener with a multiple-choice test with every interaction. These, we can do better without.

The most frequently misused communication pattern is the question. Questions can be clever, coercive or concealed ways of either offering opinions, passing judgment or manipulating others. Six of the most commonly used pseudo-questions are:

The leading question that snookers: "Don't you feel that . . . ?"; "Wouldn't you rather . . . ?" This limits or restricts the range of possible responses and leads the witness down the primrose path to make an admission or commitment that the questioner wishes, not what the responder wants. Q: "Don't you think that . . . ?" A: "No, I don't think that. . . . If you think that, I invite you to say it by speaking for yourself."

The punishing question that scolds: "Why did you say (do, try) that?" This punishes by seeking to arouse conflicts in the other or define the other person in such a way that infers there is inconsistency, contradiction or dishonesty between intention and action. Q: "Why did you do such a . . . ?" A: "I'll tell you what I want."

The demanding question that imposes: "When are you going to do something about . . . ?" This actually makes a demand or sneaks in a hidden command under the guise of an innocent request for innocuous information. Q: "When are you going to get started on . . . ?" A: "Tell me when you want it."

The dreaming question that conceals: "If you were in charge here, would you rather . . . ?" This asks for hypothetical answers. The function is to criticize in a covert way—to call a point of view impractical or irrelevant but to do it as a harmless fantasy. Q: "If you had the say around here, wouldn't you . . . ?" A: "I'd like to work with what is, now."

The needling question that provokes: "What are you waiting for?" or "What did you mean by that?" This multilevel question has a multiple choice of meanings: (1) Tell your meaning again, I'm listening. (2) What are you implying about me? (3) How dare you say that to me? (4) Can't you speak simple English, you clod? (5) You're attacking me. The needling question has as many levels as the listener may choose, and it has no single level. No matter which level the listener chooses to answer, the questioner can say, "You misunderstood me."

The trapping question that ensnares: "Didn't you once say that . . . ?" This maneuvers the other into a vulnerable position ready for the hatchet. Q: "Isn't it true that you once . . . ?" A: "Ask me about the here and now, I'm available."

I can do with a lot fewer questions. Especially those beginning with "why." "Why" questions are most often covert ways of attempted control. I want to eliminate "why" from my relationships. I will ask "what" and "how." These offer all the information I need to know to relate effectively. "Why" doesn't ask a simple question; it tends to evaluate and judge motives and intention. "What" or "how" deal with what is wanted in our relationship and how we can get it.

"Why do you always leave your things lying all over the house?" you ask.

"Why can't you pick up after yourselves?"

"Why don't you show a little interest in things?"

No one answers you. The questions accumulate around you like more litter. It's as if you go about unheard.

"Why can't I get a little cooperation?"

Your son looks up at you. "Why does everything you say begin with the word 'why'?" he asks.

"Why shouldn't it?"

"I don't know," he says, "but it feels like a trap."

"Why is that?"

"Well, you ask why, and most times there is no why. If we try to explain why, the trap snaps and you say our why was no good."

"Why is it that our kids can see through us but can't figure out why we want to know why?"

"Maybe because you don't really want to know why you want help?"

"Why are you so smart?"

"Truthing" is the word we have been using in this chapter to designate simplicity, clarity, honesty and humility in communication. Truthing seeks simplicity in its preference for single-level statements and open-ended questions. Truthing seeks clarity in its intention to not seduce, coerce, dominate or control. Truthing strives for honesty—not the so-called honesty of radical openness that ventilates without considering the impact on the receiver, but the honesty of thoughtful integrity and centered trustworthiness. Truthing prizes humility, recognizing that we know in part, see in part, understand in part. Truthing finds its core meaning in the two shortest and most powerful words (yes and no)—saying a genuine yes to the other, yes to life together in relationship, yes to moral integrity in what we are and do; speaking no to what diminishes self or other, no to what destroys relationship, no to what falls short of moral integrity.

The capacity to not only *say,* but to also *be* a clear yes and no is the quality called character. To say yes to life is good; to be that unshakable yes to the virtues of moral life is to possess character. Character is the solid stuff at the core of the self; it is the framework of personal integrity that is formed slowly and from within as one chooses to live by virtues that endure, not values that are set by context and culture. We choose virtues because they are good; values become good because we choose them. Values are a matter of personal ranking, ordering, clarifying and selecting. Virtues exist in community and are qualities of goodness that are not lost whether we can see and prize them or not. Virtues are those practices in community that one pursues because they offer internal rewards; values are those desirable external rewards that we seek as ends in themselves. Virtues point to a higher vision of life and destiny; values aim toward making the most of the pleasures of here and now. A clear yes becomes a virtue when it claims and affirms an enduring goodness that will outlive the one who chooses; a stubborn no reveals a virtue when it refuses those things that pull us away from what matters supremely, eternally. When in the moment of decision, character enables truthing—the capacity to give clear yes-signals or no-signals. Yes-signals may seem to come more easily, no-signals with more difficulty. "No" can be one of the hardest words to pronounce—face to face.

"Sure, count me in. I'll be glad to help," you say into the telephone receiver. "I like working with boys. Coaching Little League sounds fun. Right, I'll be at the meeting." You turn from the phone to face your wife's questioning eyes.

"It's just Monday and Thursday nights," you explain. "It's important for the community. I can't say no."

"If we had a boy in Little League, it would be different," your wife says. "But you don't have the time."

"I can make time for it," you say. "I just can't say no to things that ought to be done."

"But when you accept that," your wife replies, "you're saying no to having time with me and our girls; you're saying no to having time for yourself."

"Yeah, you're right. I've already got the club on Tuesdays, night school Wednesdays, bowling on Fridays, not to mention all the extras."

"When do you start saying no?" your wife asks. "With no time together, we're becoming strangers. And what time we do have we spend on working out our differences. There's no time left to just be together."

"I can't say no to this opportunity," you begin again.

"*Won't* say 'no,' " your wife corrects.

"Yeah, that's it. I'm afraid they'll quit asking me to be a part of things if I cut out once. I don't want to be passed by. But I want time with my family too. Maybe I can say no."

Clear communication gives clean, simple yes or no responses, it seeks to eliminate patterns of domination that reduce the other's freedom and increase the injustices, the personal injuries, the intrusions into another's sacred space.

"I can't say no to the boss," a junior employee explains. "I've got to do what he asks. It's the only way open to me. I have no choice."

"I have said yes to my family—to my wife and two daughters—and that rules out a lot of other yeses I might be tempted to say."

"I can't say no, I just can't." The young wife voiced her indecision over a growing friendship with her employer.

"Whatever you have to say," Jesus counseled, "let your 'yes' be a plain 'yes' and your 'no' be a plain 'no'—anything more than this has a taint of evil" (Matt. 5:37, *Phillips*).

Love is giving clear yeses and clean noes. Love gives up the concealed weapons that hide in false questions, multilevel communications, hidden messages; love makes clear statements like: I need to know. I care about you. I need you. I want your help. I want your respect.

Love opens conversation. Love sets no traps. Love plays only connecting, affirming, playful games in communication: it refuses to participate in games of control or concealment or co-opting instead of communicating with others.

Making a clear covenant for clean communication.

In all relationships, we communicate by some understanding, conscious or unconscious, of what is respectful conversation and genuine dialogue. Often the model learned in family and community is skewed, biased, slanted—toward self-protection, self-expression, self-advancement.

The following covenant is very helpful as a relational checkup on the quality of communication and equality between communicators. Try reading it back and forth with some significant other person in your life who will be willing to speak the truth about your relationship by applying these clauses to how you dialogue at your best and worst moments.

A Covenant for Clear Communication in Relationship

I pledge to you:	I promise to myself:
I want to know your world, understand your thoughts, respect your feelings.	I want you to know my world, understand my thoughts, respect my feelings.
I will honor your right to be equally heard. You are you; I want to hear you.	I will claim my privilege to be equally heard; I am I, I want to be heard.
I will respect your sole ownership for your half of our communication; I will not speak for you.	I will claim my full ownership for my side of our conversation; I will not let you speak for me.
I will listen to your thoughts and feelings, not seek to read your mind or anticipate your responses.	I will share what I think and feel, not make you guess my thoughts or suspect my real feelings.
I will not seek to limit or inhibit your free expression of needs and wants.	I will feel freely and speak frankly what I see, think, feel, want.

I want to meet you now,
in this moment
as the person you truly are.
I will not speak
to my image of you;
I cancel the demand that you
be what you were or
become what I want.

I will be with you now,
in this moment,
as the person I truly am.
I will not try
to match your image of me;
I claim the freedom
to change what I was,
choose who I am becoming.

I respect your sole responsibility:
for how you see things
and how you say things.
You are never to blame
for my responses or feelings;
You are always responsible,
You need never feel shame.
Your words and acts are yours,
I will respect them
as your choices.
I will not ask you
to take them back
to earn my acceptance.

I take full responsibility:
for how I see things
and how I say things.
I am never to blame
for your responses or feelings;
I am always responsible,
I am never to blame.
My words and acts are mine,
I will see them
as my choices.
I will stop
when they are hurtful,
modify and change them.

I will see issues
that arise between us
as two-person problems,
not just one.
I will not seek to change you,
to recreate or rework
our relationship.

I will deal only
with my part
of our two-person
process.
I will make changes
in my half of our
mutually shared relationship.

I want in no way
to hamper or hinder
your freedom to be
wholly who you are
when you are with me.

I hope in no way to
squander/surrender
my freedom to be
fully me
when I am with you.

FOR FURTHER EXPERIENCE

1. Practice listening skills to learn new ways of hearing, feeling and caring for others.

   (1) *Listen to a child.* Give your complete attention, listen with your eyes, with your full face, with your whole body by sitting at eye level. Check to see if you are truly hearing what is being said. Let your eyes gleam to affirm his or her preciousness.

   (2) *Listen to a friend.* Communicate love without putting it in words. Avoid asking questions, prompting or completing her or his sentences.

   (3) *Listen to someone you tolerate or rather dislike.* Try to really hear him or her, for a change. Become aware of your own resistance to getting close. Extend some word of understanding, appreciation or simple joy.

   (4) *Listen to yourself.* With pencil in hand, sit in silent meditation, listening. Take notes on new awareness. Let attention flow freely; see where it leads.

   (5) *Listen to God.* Listen quietly, without filling the silence with words or images. Do not take control by making requests. Remember, listening is the language of love. Listen in silence for the whisper of grace.

2. Practice simple, clear, single-level speech.

   (1) Drop all exaggeration or additional coloring of language for effect; use fewer adjectives; speak simple, clear, truthful words.

(2) Refuse all pretense—of knowing things you only guess, of being better informed or more certain of facts than you are.

(3) Live for a day without questions. If you need information, say in statement form, "I'm wondering if . . ." or "I'm wanting to know . . ."

(4) Find fresh clear ways of saying yes and no without dishonesty. Instead of "I'm sorry, but I can't" try "No, thank you. I'm wanting that time for my family."

When I become angry,
it is your fault; so change.

(You make me angry.
Your actions . . .
. . . are the cause of my pain.
So you must change . . .
and live as I prescribe;
I will blame you, ignore you
resent you, judge you
until I force you to comply,
until you make me feel good again.)

You are the cause of my distress.
You are the cause of my anger.
You must be the answer to
my pain.

If I become angry,
it is my demand for change.

(I make me angry.
My reactions . . .
. . . are the cause of my pain.
So I can change . . .
. . . how I see you.
I can choose to see you
with few or no demands,
canceling the anger;
I make me feel whole again.)

I am the owner of my feelings.
I am responsible for my demands.
I must be the answer to
my pain.

"No more bitter resentment or anger, no more shouting or slander, and let there be no bad feeling of any kind among you. Be kind to each other, be compassionate."

St. Paul, Letter to Ephesians (4:31-32, *Phillips*)

3

OWNING ANGER:

Let Both Your Faces Show

Your boss did not give you the credit for your excellent idea; your wife made a cutting remark two days ago, with no apology; your daughter didn't thank you for the little gift that you bought her; your son forgot to put the tools back in their proper place in your shop. You're feeling angry at all of them, at everything!

Anger is a demand, or sometimes a multilayered pile of demands such as:

"I demand recognition of my contribution—in a way that honors me."

"I demand an apology from you—an apology that mollifies me."

"I demand that you show appreciation for my gifts—in a way that pleases me."

"I demand that you return my tools—perfectly—just the way I keep them."

Anger is the emotion that accompanies demands. And beneath all, there is a demand that others get your demands, unquestioningly obey your demands, immediately meet your demands.

Even though the demands may seldom be put into explicit words, they are there inside the feelings, energizing the resentment. Such as: impatient anger (I demand that you do it when I want it); attention anger (I demand that you listen to me); defensive anger (I demand that you never criticize me); arrogant anger (I demand that I have the last word); controlling anger (I demand that you do what I want now); withdrawing anger (I demand that you let me go my way, do it my way).

Inside the feelings of anger or resentment that bubble up, there are layers of demands—situational demands on top, personal face-saving demands just beneath, relational longer lasting demands at the floor, and self-esteem demands in the first basement. The foundational demands—what is just and fair and right and good for all concerned and actually useful in building human community—form the bedrock beneath (only the thoughtful and truly responsible get down to this level). Freedom from being dominated by anger begins by tracking down the demands made on others. Recognizing them, naming them, seeing their source and purpose, admitting them out loud, taking responsibility for the anger demands and, finally, taking full ownership of anger. Once the anger is owned, one has a choice to (1) negotiate the demands that matter, or (2) cancel the demands that do not.

Integrity grows as one is increasingly open to facing the demands made on others. Wisdom grows as one is increasingly willing to cancel unfair, unrealistic demands. Maturity comes through freeing others to live and grow without the imposition of controlling demands.

"What if I paused to consider what I am demanding? What if I could see my layer on layer of demands clearly? What if I sorted them out to decide which are truly worth pursuing? Then I could either stick to those that are truly just, cancel those that are arrogant or self-serving, laugh at those that are childish and petulant, discard those that are unworthy of further thought and forget them.

Underneath my feelings of anger
—there are concealed expectations.
(I may not yet be aware of them myself.)
Inside my angry statements
—there are hidden demands.
(I may not yet be able to put them into words.)
Until I deal with the demands, I am doing little about it all.

Recognized or unrecognized, the demands are there. The capacity for anger, the ability to make demands, the courage to feel and follow them and the right to own and express them are essential core elements of being human, of being created as a person, of becoming a self with integrity.

Anger may be the demand that you hear me or that you recognize my worth, or that you see me as precious and worthy to be loved, or that you respect me, let go of my arm, or quit trying to take control of my life. These self-prizing demands (demands of self-respect) emerge whenever I see you as rejecting me or foresee you as about to reject me as a person of worth.

Dr. Frank Kimper, a great teacher of pastoral care, wrote of this indivisible link between self-awareness of preciousness and dignity and the demands of anger we feel when appropriate esteem and respect are withheld or denied:

> You are precious simply because you are. You were born that way. *To see that, and to be grasped by the reality of it, is to love.*
>
> Experience seems to indicate that harmonious relations are possible *only when that attitude is maintained.* This universal law has been stated in many ways—by the Jews as a simple and direct command of God, "Thou shalt love thy neighbor as thyself." The clause, "as thyself," correctly implies that *love of self is innate.* Every person senses *instinctively* the priceless nature of his own being, and reacts *reflexively* to preserve it against any threat.
>
> More specifically, each of us is automatically "defensive" in the face of perceived rejection. To be ignored as though I did not exist, or to be treated as though I were worthless, is repulsive. Instinctively, spontaneously, I react to affirm the priceless nature of my own being by becoming angry and lashing back or, feeling very hurt, by withdrawing within some protective shell to safeguard as best I can the treasured "me" I know I am.

> But my reaction to being ignored or rejected has also a second purpose: to demand by angry words or pouting that others recognize the preciousness of the self I am, and respond accordingly. Such demands fail because in making my demand I reject and ignore the very persons I want to love me; and once horns are locked in that way, the only solution is for one or the other of us (or both) to adopt an attitude of love—to see and affirm the other to be as precious as I am, *no matter what his performance.*
>
> I have never met a human being who did not have similar spiritual reflexes. Because to love one's self is a built-in reflex. Each of us was created that way.[2]

When we begin to sort through the layered muscles of demands, we find that they are attached to the skeleton of self-esteem and activated by the nerves of essential preciousness. We know (know as deep awareness) our core self-worth (it is not the reflected self-respect of my success with others, or achievement before others). We know our core self-worth as the innate preciousness of personhood, the undeniable value of the human and of co-humanity with others. We know the irreducible value of being created as a child of a loving Creator who defined His creative act as "good" and is unwilling to see any creature perish or be wasted. We know intuitively that we are worth-ful; we sense reflexively that we are precious; we feel profoundly that we are of equal value; and we respond automatically with demands when this worth-preciousness-value is ignored or injured.

Deep inside our many-layered anger lies the demand "that you recognize my worth." When you feel that another person is about to engulf or incorporate you (assuming ownership, taking you for granted, using you, absorbing you into his or her life-program), you feel angry.

Actually, you first feel anxious. "Anxiety is a sign that one's self-esteem, one's self-regard is endangered," as Harry Stack Sullivan expressed it.[3] When your freedom to be truly you is threatened, you become anxious, tense, ready for some action. Shall you escape? Or demand respect in anger? Or work out a mutual agreement? Escape may be neither possible nor practical. Agreement may seem far away since you see the other as ignoring your freedom, devaluing your worth and attempting to use you. Anger is the available option.

Anger is "the curse of interpersonal relations," Sullivan well said. It is *a curse,* because anger is instantly effective as a way of relieving the explosive pressures of anxiety. It is *a curse* because ventilation offers a temporary relief and then one must recover from the original issue as well as from the injuries caused by the outburst. It is *a curse* because when a person flashes to anger, the anger clouds recall of his or her own part in what just happened to spark the anger; oversimplifies the part the other played in the altercation; confuses awareness of what is really being demanded; and restricts ability to work toward a new agreement. So rather than being a preferred solution or even a wise choice, anger is usually the least effective option, the one that should be postponed until further conversation has been tried, the posture of demanding that is best held in abeyance until our second thoughts have been heard. It is "*a curse*" to relating.

But when our anxiety is shooting up, and the fears of being powerless before a present and irritating person become unbearable, we choose—consciously or unconsciously—to become angry.

> Anger is much more pleasant to experience than anxiety. The brute facts are that it is much more comfortable to feel angry than anxious. Admitting that neither is too delightful, there is everything in favor of anger. Anger often leaves one sort of worn out . . . and very often makes things worse in the long run, but there is a curious feeling of power when one is angry.[4]

The illusion of powerfulness (it is an illusion because force ultimately boomerangs) still prompts us to turn our arousal and anxiety into anger behavior. Check the pattern: (1) I feel keen frustration in my relationship with another; (2) I see the other person as rejecting me—my worth, my needs, my freedom, my request; (3) I am overwhelmed with demands that I only recognize in part; (4) I become suddenly and intensely anxious; (5) I blow away my anxiety with anger, which confuses things even further; (6) I may then feel guilty for my behavior and resentful of the other's part in the painful experience; (7) and I am still left holding my unresolved demands.

Anxiety is the primary emotion. It signals that a threat is received, a danger is perceived or a devaluation is "subceived" (subconsciously received) in another's response to me. It automatically triggers arousal in the release of adrenaline and puts the body on alert. It increases the level of potential feelings of all sorts and kinds: laughter can erupt as well as rage; concern for the other as well as defense of the self; caring as well as contempt.

Anger is a secondary emotion. It signals that the anxiety is now interpreted by demands, and these demands are pressing to be expressed toward the source of pain, hurt or frustration. Anger is anxiety aroused, and then interpreted by demands. The sequence is (1) anxiety arousal, (2) anger appraisal, (3) filtered by moral approval, (4) action or cancellation. In simple language, there is a burst of energy, sudden awareness of intense demands, quick judgment on what I dare say or do, and then verbal or physical expression. It looks like this: irritant→arousal; arousal →irritation; irritation→demands; demands→anger; anger →appraisal; appraisal→choice of action; action as→expression or cancellation.

If I own my anxiety and deal constructively with my demands, then my anxious arousal, my angry emotion and my moral appraisal of the situation can be used to renegotiate relationships until they are mutually satisfactory.

As you stand in the living room, looking out the window at your son's back, you're replaying the last moment's conversation.

"How stupid can you get?" you'd said to him. "You blew it again like a no-good kid. That's what you are, and you'd better shape up or you're shipping out."

There he goes, anger and rejection showing in the slump of his shoulders. "He blew it?" you ask yourself. "Well, I blew it even worse."

"How stupid can you get?" you ask again, this time the question is directed to yourself. "I get angry, I attack him personally, I put him down, I chop away at his self-esteem. I'm getting nowhere. I do the very things I hated when my dad did them. I always know better in hindsight; but when it happens, I am sightless. If I could just deal with what he's doing without attacking him. Maybe that would make a difference."

Explosive anger is powerless to effect change in relationships. It dissipates needed energies, stimulates increased negative feelings, irritates the other persons in the transaction and offers nothing but momentary discharge. Vented anger may ventilate feelings and provide instant though temporary release for tortured emotions, but it does little for relationships.

Clearly expressed anger, however, is something different. Clear statements of anger feelings and angry demands can slice through emotional barriers or communication tangles to establish contact.

When angry, I want to give clear, simple "I messages." "You messages" are most often attacks, criticisms, devaluation of the other person, labeling or ways of fixing blame. "I messages" are honest, clear, confessional. "I messages" own my anger, my responsibility and my demands without placing blame. Note the contrast between honest confession and distorted rejection.

I Messages	You Messages
I am angry.	You make me angry.
I feel rejected.	You're judging and rejecting me.
I don't like the wall between us.	You're building a wall between us.
I don't like blaming or being blamed.	You're blaming everything on me.
I want the freedom to say yes or no.	You're trying to run my life.
I want respectful friendship with you again.	You must respect me or you're out.

Anger owned and expressed in the clear descriptions of "I messages," rather than in prescriptive "you messages," becomes a positive emotion—a self-affirming emotion that responds to the threat of rejection or devaluation with these messages: (1) I am a person, a precious person, and (2) I demand that you recognize and respect me, as I pledge to recognize and respect you. The energies of anger can flow in self-affirming ways when directed by love—by the awareness of the other person's equal preciousness.

Anger energies become a creative force when they are employed (1) to change my own behavior that may have previously ignored the other's preciousness, and (2) to confront the other with his or her need to change unloving behavior. Anger energy can be directed at the cause of the anger to get at the demands

I am making, to own them and then either correct my demanding self by canceling the demand or call on the other to hear my demand and respond to how I see our relationship and what I want.

When on the receiving end of another's anger, I want to hear the anger-messages the other gives to me and check out what I am picking up as a demand. Careful listening can discern what the other is demanding, clarify it in clear statements and lead to clean confrontation. Then I have the choice of saying yes to the other's demands or saying no. I may feel angry in return, but it is more effective to experience this anger with honest "I statements" than with explosive "you statements."

Focusing your anger on the person's behavior, not on the person, frees you to stand with the other even as you stand up for your demands. The freedom to express appreciation for the other as a person, even as you explain your anger at his or her way of behaving, lets you stay in touch while getting at what you are angry about.

Maturity is manifested in learning to be angry (at behaviors) and loving (toward persons) at the same time.

Harry's been your friend for years. You could always count on him. Now you hurt him. He's turned away from, perhaps against you. Last month it was Steve. You cut him off in an angry moment; your relationship hasn't been the same. People you've been close to for years seem to be holding you at a distance.

"If they want to let me down, who needs them," you start to tell yourself, but inside you say, "I need them. I want their friendship. Yet I drive them away from me. It's like I've been carrying an overload of anger in my gut."

"I've got to talk it out with someone," you think. "I need to talk to someone about who to talk to." Who is left to ask? "Maybe my minister would listen to me—suggest where I could find out what's bugging me?"

(Memo to self: Angry for more than five days? Talk it through with another.)

"I just can't help it. It makes me angry."

"It just gets to me and touches off my temper."

"It's like something comes over me and I can't do a thing about it."

"It's other people, that's what it is. They know I've got a quick temper, and they're out to get me."

When owning your anger becomes a problem, the first sign to self or others is often the use of the word "it." "It" is the cause of untold irritation, anger, frustration, embarrassment, pain, guilt and misery. "It" is not me. "It" is this something, or someone, or some situation. When you find yourself using the word "it" as an explanation or as a scapegoat, stop. Listen to yourself. Recognize what you're doing: avoiding responsibility; sidestepping the real problem; denying ownership of your feelings, responses and actions. Internalize this thought: *Release comes not from denying but from owning who, what and where I am in my relationships.*

A great freedom comes as I own my thoughts, feelings, words and emotions: (1) I become free to choose my actions, and (2) I become free to choose my reactions.

My actions are mine; your actions are yours. I am responsible for my behavior; you are responsible for yours. In reality, no one can make another angry. If I become angry at you, I am responsible for that reaction. (I am not saying that anger is wrong. It may well be the most appropriate and loving response that I am aware of at that moment.) But *you* do not make me angry. *I* make me angry at you. It is not the only behavior open to me. There is no situation in which anger is the only possible response. If I become angry (and I may, it's acceptable), it's because I choose to respond with anger. I might have chosen kindness, irritation, humor or many other alternatives (if I had been aware of these choices). There is no situation that commands us absolutely. For example, I have the choice to respond to another's threat with blind obedience, with silent passivity, with vocal refusal, with firm resistance or with anger, if that seems appropriate. When childhood experiences are limited, a person may mature with a limited set of behaviors familiar or practiced. Some have only two ways of coping with another's attack—anger or submission. If these are the only ways modeled by the parents or the family, they may be the only awareness-choices in the person's behavioral repertoire.

If I have grown enough in life so that more than one pattern of behavior is available to me, then I can freely select the responses that seem most appropriate to the situation—anger or patience; toughness or gentleness; clear confrontation or warm, caring support. I want to be able to respond in any of these. I am "response-able" for choosing my responses to you; for the way I react to you; for how I see you. And from the way I see you—friendly or hostile, accepting or rejecting, welcoming or threatening—emerge my feelings. Feelings are the energies that power the way I choose to see you or perceive you. I am responsible for how I see you—and from that, for the way I feel about you.

You cannot make me angry; I choose to be angry. You cannot make me discouraged or disgusted or depressed. These are my choices. You cannot make me hate. Hate is a choice. You cannot make me jealous. I must choose to be comparative and possessive in jealousy. I experience all these and more on all too many occasions, but I am responsible for those actions or reactions. I make the choice. And I am free to choose loving responses. I am free to choose trusting replies. I am free to react in concerned, understanding ways if I choose to see the other person as precious, as valuable, as worthy of love because he or she is equally loved of God.

We look to Jesus as the primary exemplar for our loving relationships; He is equally clear about the other side of that love in His expression of the urgency of clean anger. Here is a case in point worth thoughtful consideration:

Anger erupted in a place of worship, the synagogue.

A handicapped man with paralysis of arm and hand came asking Jesus for healing. The religious leaders are (1) looking on with malice, (2) anticipating that Jesus may break the ceremonial blue laws against doing a service for another on the Sabbath, and (3) hoping for some such infraction of the law so that they can charge Him with illegal, irreligious, irresponsible action.

Jesus avoids neither the man in need nor His own critics.

"Stand up and come out here in front," He says to the man.

Then He turns to the Pharisees. He is aware of their demands—demands characteristic of many religious leaders through the centuries—(1) that principles come before the pain of persons, (2) that religious piety be honored above the needs of a brother, (3) that legalistic obedience is more important than human life and love for others. Jesus focuses their demands in the kind of question-statements they were so fond of debating. "What is truly right, just, good? To do good or do evil on the Sabbath? To save life or destroy it?" But in acting so, He is clearly confronting and refusing their demands. There is silence. (As an answer, silence is often violence.)

Jesus is deeply hurt at their inhumanity.

He looks at them in anger. His look sweeps from one face to another. His demand is clear. Be human. Be loving. Care about people. Be just. Respect this man's needs. See him as precious. Act toward him in co-humanity.

Then Jesus does the responsible, loving, caring, truly just thing. "Stretch out your hand," He says to the man. The man stretches it out, and it is as sound as the other (Mark 3:1-6, paraphrased from *Phillips*).

That is an instance of clear, focused, creative, controlled, dynamic anger. In the face of persons who reduce reality to simple definitions, who see half of experience as acceptable and the other half as expendable in clearly defined categories, Jesus offers a wider view of compassionate grace for whole persons, for transforming their whole experience, for growing toward a wholeness that offers healing for our brokenness in the face of persons and systems that reject us.

He does not model a maturity won by cutting off one-half of the emotional spectrum and rejecting all negative feelings in pursuit of the positive. As a whole person in relationships, He risked sharing both sides of Himself. He offered an invitation to us to be open with both our negatives (honest anger) and our positives (affirming love), to let both faces show. There are two sides in everyone. Both sides are important. Both are acceptable. Both are precious. Both can be loved.

We prefer to think that God wants our very best and only our best; that God will have nothing to do with weakness, timidity or fears. Not so. God accepts weakness as well as strength, fear as well as confidence, anger as well as gentleness. God invites us to become whole persons. To deny and repress everything on the negative side is to also stifle and crush the full expression of the positive side. There is danger in abusing and misusing others with positive emotions and actions—love, kindness, gentleness, tolerance, sweetness—just as there is the threat of cutting and destroying others with negative responses—anger, harshness, criticism, irritation. To be engulfed and incorporated by a smothering love, all sweet gentleness and I'm-only-trying-to-help-you-it's-for-your-own-good kindness may be more treacherous than harsh, crisp frankness. It is more possible to refuse frankness than to resist an all-absorbing sticky mass of cotton candy love.

As we know and experience the love of God, acceptance reaches out to include both sides of us. God knows the best and worst about us and loves us anyway. We can be aware of feelings of anger. (We are accepted.) We can own resentments, hate, hostility. (We are loved.) We can discover new ways of experiencing both negative and positive feelings. (We are free to grow.) We can be angry in creative, loving, caring ways. (We can see it modeled in Jesus.)

As a paradigm for a balanced experience and expression of love and anger, consider the following set of attitudes toward self and toward the other. Read it multiple times, thinking of the significant relationships in your life. What if you lived in this way with everyone in your personal world?

I do love me.
I love my freedom
to be who I am.
I love my drive
to be all I can be.
I love my right
to differ from you.
I love my need
to be related to you.

I am free to accept or to refuse
your wants
your requests
your expectations
your demands.
I can say yes.
I can say no.
I am not in this world
to live as you prescribe.
The thoughts I think,
The words I speak,
The actions I take,
The emotions I feel—
they are mine.
For them I am
fully responsible.
I am not responsible for you.
I will not be responsible
to you.
I want to be responsible
with you.

I also, I equally, love you.
I respect your freedom
to be who you are.
I admire your drive
to be all you can be.
I recognize your right
to be different from me.
I appreciate your need
to be related to me.

You are free to accept or to refuse
my wants
my requests
my expectations
my demands.
You can say yes.
You can say no.
You are not in this world
to live as I prescribe.
The thoughts you think,
The words you speak,
The actions you take,
The emotions you feel—
they are yours.
For them I am
in no way responsible.
You are not responsible for me.
You need not be responsible
to me.
You can be responsible
with me.

FOR FURTHER EXPERIENCE

1. Read Psalm 40 to observe David's frank honesty with God as his feelings flow out. List the feelings—from depression to release, elation, fear, joy in helping others, anger, resentment, trust and final impatience. What permission does this offer you?

2. To put your negative feelings into words and own them with integrity, complete these phrases in at least five ways:

   I get angry when . . .

   And my most characteristic behavior is . . .

   And afterward I feel . . .

   But what I really want is . . .

3. To get in touch with the demands inside your anger, end this sentence in five ways:

   When I become angry, my demands are . . .

4. To explore new behaviors in conflict situations, finish these lines as a creative rehearsal of new ways of responding to others:

   When I am anxious and aroused, I will delay the move to anger by . . .

   When I am in conflict and I become angry, I will take time out by . . .

Of course I differ from you.
(To differ is not to reject.)
Sometimes I disagree with you.
(To disagree is not to attack.)
When necessary, I will confront you.
(To confront is to complement.)
When confronting, I will first connect.
(To confront well we must first be connected.)
When it matters, I will invite change.
(To change is to grow.)

We can grow through conflict.
(And confrontation is a healthy part.)

So let's explore where we differ and complement.
(If we agree on everything, one of us is unnecessary.)

"Love in all sincerity. . . . Care as much about each other as about yourselves."

St. Paul, Letter to Romans (12:9,16, *NEB*).

4

INVITING CHANGE:

Careful Confrontation

When unchallenged, human beings often become self-centered, individualistic, self-absorbed. When unchallenged, human groups tend to drift, wander or stagnate. When unchallenged, relationships tend to repeat, become routine, become stale or stuck. Life without challenge and confrontation is directionless, aimless, passive; or selfish, self-serving, empty.

Confrontation, uncomfortable as it can be, is a gift.

Confrontation is a necessary stimulation to jog one out of mediocrity or to prod one back from extremes. Life without the balance provided by constructive tensions is flat, finally boring, undesirable.

Confrontation is an art to be learned.

To affront is easy. Examples for being caustic, critical, cutting are available in abundance. Few of us need any lessons to learn how to tell people off. We can do it while asleep.

To confront, and to do it well, is hard. For many persons, there have not been good examples in their family or friendships that modeled how to be candid, clear and confrontive without being uncaring. Indeed, such balanced, genuine people are unusual if not truly rare. Who of us could not use constructive help in learning how to confront in a way that doesn't frustrate or alienate?

When a relationship needs to be reworked, one of the first things required is some new data on the needs and interests of both parties. Usually the data needed is already there in the relationship—one or the other has a good clue—but they are in no position to offer it, or they do not dare risk the threat of sharing it, or they just don't know how to begin. The ability to offer the amount useful to the other, not the amount available at the moment, is wisdom that comes from experience.

Sometimes in crisis or emergency we need to put a lot on the table at once. When a situation calls for a great deal of self-disclosure, it must be done with high sensitivity. The ability to offer another a maximum amount of information about another's part in relationship with a minimum amount of threat to that relationship is a skill to be learned bit upon bit, new response added to old response.

Giving another feedback on how he or she is coming on is never easy or simple; but when it is offered in a context of caring, supportive acceptance, it can be heard (grudgingly, of course), and in time put to use. If it is offered brashly or rashly; it can be astoundingly difficult to hear, interpret and put to use when it sounds like blunt, insensitive, non-supportive rejection.

Hearing confrontation from another is never easy, but it is less difficult if one is certain that the other respects, values, cares—in spite of all differences; but when respect is unclear and caring is unexpressed, one can feel fed up with another's feedback as soon as it begins.

Caring comes first; confrontation follows. A context of caring can be created when a person is truly *for* another, genuinely concerned *about* another, authentically related *to* another. The content of such caring is, however, not a blank check approval of the other. The core of true caring is a *clear invitation to grow*, to become what he or she truly is and can be, to move toward maturity. Accepting, appreciating and valuing another is an important part of relationship, but these attitudes may or may not be *caring.*

The crucial element that defines caring, that makes acceptance and appreciation rise to become authentic care, is this: Does the appreciation foster growth? Does it invite maturing? Does it set another more free to be? Does it invite the unfolding and fulfillment of the other person's development as a person?

Caring is a commitment to create a context of support for another, to be a voice of encouragement to another, to stand in solidarity with another. And the measure of its effectiveness is not the caregiver's intentions (our intentions are always good, eh?) but the receiver's perception of what is being given. If the caregiver is meeting her own needs, attending to her own goals, "scratching where she itches," it is rarely perceived as caring. When the caring person is attuned to the needs and direction of the other and offers support and feedback that connect with the other's present position, as well as point to where they could be going, the information will more likely be heard, and perhaps even be useful.

A context of caring must come before confrontation.
A sense of support must be present before criticism.
An experience of empathy must precede evaluation.
A basis of trust must be laid before one risks advising.
A floor of affirmation must undergird any assertiveness.
A gift of understanding opens the way to disagreeing.
An awareness of love sets us free to level with each other.

Building solidarity in relationships with others—through caring, support, empathy, trust, affirmation, understanding and love—provides a foundation for the more powerful actions of confrontation, criticism, evaluation, counsel, assertiveness, disagreement and open leveling with each other.

Leading with power violates love. Leading with love humanizes power. Power without love is ruthless. Love without power is helpless. Power grounded in and shaped by love strengthens both giver and receiver. *Loving power is the heart of authentic relating.*

"Is this guy going to talk forever?" you wonder as the committee meeting drags on past the scheduled adjournment time. The chairman has ignored three suggestions that you deal with the group's stated agenda and is going on and on with one of his personal concerns. If this were his first filibuster, you might overlook it as you've done several times already.

You check your watch, resisting the urge to shake it and put it to your ear.

"I'll sit this one out," you think, "and then find a good reason to drop off this committee in the future."

Or you could plead ill, right now, indeed you *are* feeling sick of it all, then excuse yourself and leave.

The impulse to be suddenly frank rises within you. "You've told us more than we need or want to know about X. I think we are at a good stopping place. I move that we adjourn," you're tempted to say, but you care a bit too much to put him down.

He is asking for support; what he needs is someone to care. He is demanding attention; what he needs is to be connected responsibly with someone. Everyone here is totally disconnected from him.

"I'm not sure I was aware how important this issue is to you," you say gently. "We are running short of time this evening. I believe we could finish our work in the time we have left if we focus carefully. Let's give it a try."

Confrontation invites another to change but does not demand it. The confronter does not make the continuation of the friendship hang on a change of behavior in the confrontee. Acceptance of the other person is not connected to agreement or disagreement. Acceptance does not exclude differing; it frees us to differ more fully, frankly, effectively.

Wholesale approval of another suggests that one is either totally unconcerned or radically uninvolved with the other. Cheap approval can be lavished on anyone at any time, to any extent.

But caring requires that one get interested in the direction the other's life is taking and offer real immediate involvement.

You must care a good deal to risk challenging another person's routine behaviors. It is a deliberate and sometimes dangerous choice. If you love, you level. If you value another, you volunteer the truth.

Confrontation is not a matter of tact, diplomacy and smoothness of tongue. It is basically simplicity of speech, empathy in attitude and honesty in response (to sum up into one sentence the guidelines for giving effective feedback).

The following skills for offering clear confrontation are given as basic guidelines. They are ways of practicing simplicity, honesty and empathy. To be free to value another equally as oneself, to seek to see from the other's point of view, is to offer confrontation in a way that is immediately useful without being stressful.

- When confronting, focus your feedback *NOT on the actor BUT on the action.* Comment not on the person *but* on the behavior in question. To criticize the *actor* in a less than desirable way stimulates feelings of rejection; to critique the *action* affirms the other's freedom to change, encourages the person to disconnect from the behavior in question, and invites him to consider another option in future situations. Example: "When someone criticizes people not present, as you were doing a moment ago, I get uptight. I'd encourage you to say what you have to say to the person."

- When confronting, focus your feedback *NOT on your conclusions BUT on your observations.* Comment not on what you think, imagine or infer, *but* on what you have actually seen or heard. Statements of observation (fact) can be made only after observing, must be limited to what one has observed, and can be made only by the observer. Statements of inference (conclusions or rumor) can go beyond observation, can be made by anyone, anytime, to anyone. These involve only degrees of probability, evoke immediate defensiveness in the receiver, and offer more confusion than clarification even when the content is accurate. Example: "You're not looking at me and not answering when I speak. Please give me both attention and an answer."

- When confronting, focus your feedback *NOT on judgments BUT on descriptions.* Comment not on how you would label the other's behavior as nice or rude, right or wrong, good or bad, *but* on clear, accurate description in as neutral language as possible. When a value judgment is received there is a momentary break in contact. A slow-motion replay of a videotape will show that the recipient's eyes close at the instant the loaded words are received, a frown creases the forehead. For a moment, communication is broken. Description offers no such effect. Example: "I'm aware that you reply to my requests for information with silence. Please tell me what this means."

- When confronting, focus your feedback *NOT on quality BUT on quantity.* Comment not on the character, trait or classification (qualities) of the other person, *but* on the amount of the feeling, expression or action (quantity). Use adverbs (which tell how much) rather than adjectives (which tell what kind of). Use terms denoting "more-or-less" (quantity) rather than "either-or" categories (quality). "You talked considerably more than others," not "You were a loudmouth." "You have asked for and received more of my time than any other student," not "You are clinging, dependent and always demanding time."

- When confronting, focus your feedback *NOT on advice and answers BUT on ideas, information and alternatives.* Comment not with instructions on what to do with the data you have to offer *but* with the data, the facts, the additional options. To increase another's alternatives is to enrich another. The more open possibilities available, the less likely one is to move to a premature solution. Example: "I've several other options I want to report, which you may have thought about, but let me run them by you once again."

- When confronting, focus your feedback *NOT on the amount available within you as giver BUT on the amount useful to the receiver.* Comment not to ventilate and get release from your pent-up feelings *but* to give something of worth to the other, something helpful to another. Offer it; do not seek to force it on the other. Report what the receiver can best use rather than all you would like to say. If you overload the other's channels, you only block, frustrate and may do more harm than good. Example: "I think that blaming your mother for your struggles blocks your growth," not "As long as you keep blaming your parents, you are admitting you are still a child, like the last nine . . ."

- When confronting, focus feedback *NOT on the easiest time and place to suit your own schedule BUT on the best time and the optimal situation for the receiver.* We schedule all conflicts either by conscious choice or unconscious hunch. To choose time and place purposefully allows us to have the best interests of the other truly in the foreground. Example: "I'd like a few minutes for conversation after dinner. Shall we go for a short walk?"

- When confronting, focus feedback *NOT on "why" BUT on "what" and "how."* "Why" critiques values, motives, intents. "Why" sits in judgment. "What" and "how" relate to observable actions, behaviors, words and tone of voice. "Why" gets into trying to decipher cause and effect. "Why" starts with being historical and ends in becoming hysterical. Example: "Here is where we are. Let's examine it. Now is when we are meeting, let's encounter each other," rather than "Why are you still reviewing the past and trying to fix blame for what happened? If you succeed in finding who is at fault, what then?"

These eight skills are helpful in separating the issues from the person, of learning how to be clear on concerns while staying connected to the person, of being hard on issues and soft on people. To develop the ability to use eight out of eight in offering another confrontive feedback is not so hard as it may seem at first survey. The key to building skills in giving constructive feedback is to focus on the action, on observations, on description, on quantity, on information, on alternatives, on the amount useful, on the best time and place, dealing with what and how in the here and now. The pitfalls are the direct opposites, so learn not to focus on the actor, on conclusions, on judgments, on qualities, on advice, on the amount of feedback you may have available, on seizing the easiest time and place, or on pursuing why, why, why.

Simple, honest, empathic speech can achieve most of these positive goals and eliminate many of the pitfalls.

It's the end of a usual evening. You're stretched out in your favorite chair when your wife pulls up beside you, pad and pencil in hand.

"May I read you the collected sayings of Chairman You-know-who from the moment you got home until now?" (Focus on behavior.)

"Yeah, if it's all that good," you say.

"Okay. 5:35, 'Hi, I'm home.'

6:20, 'Hamburger again? That all we can afford?'

7:14, 'How come the paper's wet?'

8:30, 'Switch the channel. That's a lousy show.' " (Clear reporting of observations.)

"Look," you say, "you wanted to talk? Why didn't you marry a minister?"

"Funny you should ask, I suspect I married a monk. You walk in the door, say 'Hi,' then take a vow of silence. All I want is a little companionship," she says. (Clear description.)

"No, you missed something," you reply. "I walk in, say 'Hi.' You give me that I'm-burned-up-that-you're-late-again look and I know that silence is my only safety, so I shut up." (Blaming the actor while pretending it is describing an action.)

"When you withdraw," she says, "I want some response out of you, so I do a little prodding."

The honesty hits you. The two of you are saying the same thing. But each is saying that the other starts it. Maybe it's one continuous cycle. I nudge, you withdraw; I nudge, you withdraw; so I nag, you withdraw even further.

"Honey," you say, "who cares which came first—your prodding or my silence. We're stuck in this cycle. How can we break it?"

"I guess I could say something warm instead of digging at you."

"Okay. And I'll say what I really want instead of withdrawing."

Clear description of what is happening between two people can often clarify a confusing routine or blow the cover on an old game.

Clear observation of what we are doing to each other and how we are doing it can free us to see an old situation with new eyes.

Clear expression of what is thought and felt by each person can clear the air and free us both to zero in on what is needed for more harmonious relating.

Clear negotiation of what each wants of the relationship can correct past injustices and choose ways of responding to each other that are mutually satisfactory.

The central goal in all of these is to care, to manifest concern for the other and to deepen the involvement each has in the other.

Caring confrontation is characterized by this constant concern for the other's self-respect as well as for asserting one's own needs for greater respect. When the other's emotional safety and security are as important to me as my own, caring will be unquestionably present.

In the previous chapter, we explored five ways of working through conflict. This chapter has focused on the key skill of blending caring and confrontation in what we are calling "a third way" that seeks to bring together the strong commitment to relationship with a concern for goals, values and ends. A 9/9 Third way seeks to build a strong floor of connected supportive relationship while also risking sharing vision and values. The more common process is to alternate between an acceptant relationship of caring until it is intolerable, then to explode in confrontation in a way that is so contradictory, the person no longer believes the past and becomes angry at the feedback being offered in the present.

The ambivalence in the one who is finally confronting—who swings from acceptance to disagreement—now triggers ambivalence in the recipient. This is all contained in the little word "but." The feedback usually goes something like this: "I really like working with you, ***but*** when you start criticizing people so ruthlessly, I wonder what you say about me behind my back and I don't trust you." No one remembers anything said—no matter how affirming and supportive—before the word "but." Once it breaks into the feedback, the ambivalence of the speaker evokes even greater ambivalence in the listener. Any hope that the caring context implied in the first words will give support for what follows is in vain. The word "but" is a perfect and infallible eraser. The word "but" hits the delete key on the listener's keyboard. The word "but" signals that what follows is the important part of the message. "And" is the connecting word that brings caring and confronting into "care-fronting" balance. When the other hears, "I am committed to our working relationship, I am glad we are on the same team, ***and*** I think we can achieve more of our goals if we . . ." there is no ambivalence, no set-up, no lather-before-shave, no splitting of communication and, therefore, of relationship.

Caring and confronting unite in creating connection, not the disconnect that comes as one offers "caring, ***but, but, but*** I have something to say in confrontation." The ability to unite both concerns—commitment to relationship and commitment to goals—into one authentic process of negotiation reduces threat, eliminates manipulation, avoids splitting and communicates wholeness in the I-You encounter.

"You quit your job? But that's stupid," you snap at your son. "You had a good thing going after school and now you drop it."

"Yeah, well, I just could not tolerate working there anymore. I decided to quit, to split," he says.

"I'd have given a lot to have a job like that when I was in school, but you just threw it away? You'll never amount to anything."

"Not if that is the only way '*to amount to anything*.' "

"It's a way to be responsible with a job, with an employer, with real life."

"You don't understand; I'm not sure you try to understand."

He hits a nerve. You are good at confronting—from your point of view. But not so good at caring about what he is thinking and feeling. You're stuck at a familiar impasse: You're writing him off; he walks out. You're predicting failure; he tunes you out. You're keeping score on his mistakes; he fights back. You're dishing it out; he spites you in return.

"You're right. I didn't ask why you quit. I thought it would get us into another cycle of blame."

"Probably would, but I'm willing to try. I quit because I just couldn't super-size the fast-food crap any longer. If you haven't noticed, I've become a vegetarian since working there. I can't stand the smell of grease. And I'm pushing it at the window on every gullible customer. 'Do you want fries with that? Would you like nacho cheese on the fries? Was that a triple burger or a double? With extra mayo and super-sauce? With cheese?' I can't do it any longer."

"I've never heard you talk about this before."

"Calling planet Earth. I've talked about the classes on environment that I'm taking this semester. I told you all at dinner last Sunday about the youth class on ethics of food. I leave books lying around on stuff that matters to me. These are not just entertainment or education; they are what matters."

"Let me see if I got it. You quit your job because of a . . . a matter of conscience?"

"Sounds weird to you as a lawyer? Yes, you got it."

"No, it sounds pretty good to me."

"Are you all right, Dad? Should you be standing? Maybe you'd better sit down?"

Out of both good and bad experiences of giving and receiving confrontation, I offer the following five guidelines.

Confront caringly. Confront only after experiencing real care for the other; confront primarily to express real concern for another. Unless the other matters more to you than your situational discomfort or disagreement, the confrontation will not be of use.

Confront gently. Do not offer more than the relationship can bear. Do not draw out more than you have put into the friendship. Ask, what have I invested? What trust do we have in the relational account? Am I willing to cash in all my chips on this issue?

Confront constructively. Take into consideration any possible interpretations of blaming, shaming, punishing. These are the negative side effects of most confrontations. They will overshadow what you intend to communicate even when your intentions are clearly expressed in what you thought were credible ways.

Confront respectfully. Respect the other's intentions as always good. For the average person, motives are inevitably mixed, and the conscious intention is invariably good when rightly understood. Little is to be gained in impugning motives or evaluating another's hopes, wishes, goals.

Confront clearly. Report what is fact (observation), what is feeling (emotion), what is hypothesis (conclusion). Sharpen your skills of differentiating between facts and their interpretations. Do not confuse them. Do not state an interpretation as though it were a fact.

But do confront. It is not a matter of "if" I can afford to be real with you, but "when." To care is to be there for another. Care enough and you will confront.

Giving effective, affirmative and assertive feedback or confrontation. The goal in giving feedback to another in relationships—personal, working or group relationships—is to offer the maximum amount of information with a minimum of threat to the recipient and the relationship. We do this most effectively by decreasing those things that are non-affirmative and seeking to strengthen the positive bonding between us as we explore differences.

Affirmative Confrontation	Non-affirmative Confrontation
Focus feedback on actual behavior, not on the person; criticize specific visible, present or recent actions.	Focus feedback on the person; criticize the person and generalize to comment on the inadequacies of the personality.
Offer feedback in simple supportive descriptions and observations that show as little bias as possible.	Offer feedback with judgments, labels and conclusions that analyze motives, intentions and immaturity.
Express feedback by talking of quantity, using terms that speak of more and less, relating to actions and intensity such as, "You talked considerably more than . . ."	Express feedback by defining quality, using terms that speak of good and bad, of traits and basic personality patterns, "You were a dominating narcissist . . ."
Report feedback as alternatives that will increase the other's options to choose and leave them free to use or not use it.	Report feedback as advice and answers that tell them what to do about their problems, how to change personality.
Give feedback in the amount useful, not the amount you may have available. Do not overload or be insensitive to the other's optimum time to receive data.	Give feedback in the amount available whether or not useful or appropriate at the present moment. Say what you need to say for your release.
Focus feedback on what and how, here and now, with useful, clearly identified, changeable behavioral suggestions. Care about the person, their self-respect, integrity, dignity and personal strengths. Energize and encourage.	Focus feedback on why; keep asking why in ways that question, critique, judge or shame the other for failing. Confront about what annoys, irritates, and reveals insecurity or weakness. Deflate and set straight.

FOR FURTHER EXPERIENCE

Your task is to mentally construct the five alternative responses to the following episode.

Case: For years you have been unable to say no to the heavy demands on your time from a charitable organization that you have gladly supported. Now the chairperson is calling on you again to attempt to pressure you into heading up the annual fund drive, even though this is one of your least favorite tasks. When you refuse, she redoubles her efforts to persuade you. You feel like saying:

"How can you ask me to do this again after all the time I donated last year? Quit twisting my arm. Can't you be more considerate? I'm so tired of all this load of jobs, deadlines and obligations. Count me out, mark me off your list and get someone who has nothing better to do." Reflect a moment and try other options.

1. Confront caringly. (Try: *I've been concerned about your organization, as my last year's schedule will show. This year I'm guarding my time carefully and will not be available.*)
2. Confront gently. (Try: *I do appreciate your thinking of me in choosing someone for the assignment; however, I'm reserving that block of time for myself and my family this year.*)
3. Confront constructively. (Try: *I'm not available this year; I hope you have persons on your list who will be eager to help this year.*)
4. Confront respectfully. (Try: *I can hear how much you are needing volunteers this year. I won't be helping on this round. I hope you are able to gather a staff to help.*)
5. Confront clearly. (Try: *I have already said no in four clear ways. I think I'm able to continue to do that under any persuasion or pressure. I can appreciate how much you want to find volunteers, however, I am not volunteering.*)

To be trusted
Trust.
If you wait
until trust is deserved,
you wait forever.
Trust now.
Someone is waiting
to trust in return.

"Love knows no limit to its endurance,
no end to its trust,
no fading of its hope; it
can outlast anything."

St. Paul, Letter of First Corinthians (13:7-8, *Phillips*)

5

GIVING TRUST:

A Two-Way Venture of Faith and Risk

"Don't trust anyone over 30," warned those who thought they had discovered that honesty ended at 29.

Then 20-year-olds began to note how hard it was getting through to the 25s.

"They don't get it," they complained. "We don't read each other anymore."

Then the 18-year-olds began to sense how dense were the guys past 20.

No sooner had Miss 18 pointed this out than she was deflated by the 15-year-olds.

"Just because they can drive, they think they oughta be able to vote and drink."

That's where the 12-year-olds chipped in.

"Teenagers are terrible," they said. "Have you tried talking to thirteeners? They say anybody that doesn't listen to them can lump it!"

The 10-year-olds spoke up.

"Twelve-year-olds are a bunch of spoiled brats; they are high on puberty, voices changing, figures developing and they want to tell all kids how to do everything. You can't trust them."

The five-year-olds finally got in a word. "First graders cause all the problems. Just because they've got an education and can read they think the world is their Twinkie."

Now the kindergartners are getting it from the nursery school tykes.

"So they can ride without training wheels, big deal." And the toddlers in their terrible twos find the threes and fours infuriating.

"So they're potty trained? They're hardly out of diapers and they think they're big stuff." And the one-year-olds are still working at achieving basic trust. So who's to be trusted?

Basic trust is the primal learning in the life of every child. Basic trust is the foundation for all subsequent learning. And it remains the key, core, crucial emotion in all human relationships. Trust undergirds, interconnects, integrates, interrelates all the other emotions and affections. Trust is the root emotion. In stress we fall back through the levels of fidelity, competence, purpose, will, hope until we encounter the fundamental ground of our being: trust. These are the stages of growth and development as seen by Erik Erikson.[5] His work is foundational to many other thinkers in psychology, education, theology and clinical practice. He begins from the foundational understanding of the importance of trust. However, he does not speak of it as an optimistic Pollyanna stance of positive thinking. For him, trust must be balanced by mistrust. The child learns to trust what is safe, satisfying, secure in its environment, as well as to mistrust what is frightening, painful, lonely and anxiety arousing. Both of these learnings are necessary; both crucial to healthy growth; both must stand in balance if the first virtue of human development is to appear—hope. Hope contains both trust and mistrust in tension. Hope is the confident expectation of something desired in the face of the possibility that it may not happen; hope is the earnest longing for what can appear in spite of past experiences when it did not; hope is the certainty that good will come even in the face of things looking bad. So trust in what can be, persisting in spite of the fear that it might not be, emerges as hope.

Trust is the foundation of all effective human relating. Trust is the core orientation toward life, not an acquired personal quality, character trait or Christian virtue to be possessed and prized.

Trust is the basic floor of all relationships that dare to take the risks that result in reliability; the basis of all honesty that creates webs of enduring loyalty, of every expression of human goodness that is exchanged with others in genuineness. Trust is the basic stuff of all relationships.

Because trust is the necessary basis for communication about our differences and constructive working through of our differences, understanding what it is and how it works in relationships is basic to all conflict management. Confrontation without a floor of trust is useless. Confrontation with a solid foundation of trust builds rapport, opens understanding, earns respect and will be heard. Trust with integrity is trust with its eyes open. It is trust that cares enough to confront the other responsibly and requests the other to assume his or her responsibility to be equally honest, frank and out in the open with what he or she is choosing to do. Such trust willingly accepts apologies, forgives the past, cancels old debts and gives the other his or her future back again.

Since trust is the primal familial emotion, we will explore it in this chapter primarily in the parent-parent and parent-child settings of conflict. Observations offered as to its nature are equally applicable elsewhere. For example, trust between intimates results in *open love*—clear messages of affection and fidelity and *open honesty*—clear statements of what I want, how I feel, how I behave and act in all my relationships. Love and honesty in relationships are dependent on the foundation of trust because trust is a relational, two-way experience. It is circular. Continuous. Reciprocal. It is trust—*between*. It enables the loving honest exchange of two or more persons as they interact and interrelate. Trust underlies all.

"I trust you." When I hear—or sense—that message from another person, I feel capable, respected and in some way accepted and loved.

"I don't trust you." When I receive that message from someone important to me, I feel suspected, sidelined, disliked, perhaps cut off and rejected.

If being trusted is so significant to our own sense of well-being and self-esteem, then a climate of trust is one of the most crucial elements in life, in families and homes. Trust, breathed in an atmosphere of love, nourishes life like oxygen. Distrust tightens the chest with anxiety, burns in the throat like smog, tears the eyes with its acidity and poisons the whole person.

Test it for yourself. Close your eyes. Withdraw into yourself for a moment. Say, "Someone important no longer trusts me. Perhaps I do not deserve to be trusted. If others join in this suspicion, I will be rejected as untrustworthy." What do you feel? There's a narrowing of the chest, isn't there? A tightness in breathing. You want to draw in air but it comes hard. That's anxiety. That's how it feels when we are not trusted. A breath of fresh trust can give a person enough life to go on for days. But deny a child—or a parent—or any person—of trust and he or she starves on the stale air of suspicion and rejection. One cannot live without trust. Deprive another of it and he'll seek it elsewhere, getting it wherever he can find it. Or she may come to the point where she says, "I trust no one. No one but me—myself." That too is death. We need trust to be human. To refuse to trust is to do violence to human personhood.

Giving trust is the central task of parenting. To withhold it is to deprive an emerging person of the core need of its being. To withhold trust as a means of coercing conformity (which incidentally does not work, no matter how commonly it is tried) is to say: "Until you measure up to my demands, I withhold the breath of life-nourishing trust from you. When you earn it again, when I decide you deserve it, I may give it back."

"They're a bunch of little devils, the kids they run around with," your husband says as your daughters back their VW bug out of the drive. "Who knows what they're up to? They have friends that are sleeping around, popping pills, smoking pot. Either you're with me—and we crack down on them—or you're with them . . ."

You're in a real bind. You love your husband. You want to stay in touch with him. But you love your daughters too. Yes, some of the kids your daughters know have serious problems, and some are great kids with good values. If you write them all off, you're writing off your daughters' respect and trust as well. Nothing can persuade you to feel so angrily judging as your husband wants you to be.

"I'm not going to reject either side," you tell yourself. "Both my husband and my daughters need me. I need them. I won't let his suspicions and anger stop me from giving trust to the girls, nor will I let myself be cut off from him. My daughters' problems are not going to come between us."

(Memo to self: Few situations in relationship can be reduced to simple either/or ends. Both sides must be heard, and in large part, respected and honored.)

But what if a spouse, a son or a daughter betrays your trust? What if your trust is abused? Should trust be extended only when clearly deserved? Trust includes two aspects: faith and risk. We believe in the other's trustworthiness, step one, so we risk, step two. The risk is validated by faithful behavior, step three, so we risk more, step four. It is like walking, one foot after the other—faith and risk, further faith and greater risk, solid faith and larger risks.

A climate of mutual trust develops out of mutual freedom to risk sharing personal thoughts and feelings and to listen to the other's private world with gentle respect. This frees both to share hopes and dreams and become acquainted with the other's plans and goals. Out of this comes the willingness to talk about experiences in the present and experiment in being more genuine and open with others. This frees the other to tell about their successes and failures and what they are exploring next. This two-way process is like a dance as well as like walking together. The steps include openness and self-disclosure as a part of risk, and shared commitments and goals as a part of faith. It is a dance of trust. As faith grows in each that the private will be respected and the personal will be honored, then both parties move forward together in a trust walk.

The key thing is that we do not talk about trusting or not trusting another. That contains too many elements of suspicion and fear, of evaluation and rejection. We talk about risk. In mediation, it is never wise to ask if you can trust the other party or how much are you willing to trust the adversary. The answer is virtually always guarded, defensive, understandably cautious. One asks instead, "How much are you willing to risk?" As risks are taken and reciprocal risks are returned, faith in the other's good will increases. This is trust, the union of faith and risk.

In good parenting, you do not say, "I do not think I can trust you again," or "You have betrayed our trust and you're going to have to earn it again." Instead you might say something like, "I think we risked too much by giving you the car and a credit card without looking carefully at the pressures you would face from your peer group." "We put you in a vulnerable spot. We would be wiser to risk less at the moment."

And as the trust level rises, the willingness to risk being open to new things with each other increases, and faith in each other's predictability grows too. The two go hand in hand. Faith and risk. Confidence and wider freedoms. Positive assurance and greater possibilities. Comfort and vulnerability. Acceptance and honesty. Each is advanced by the other; each is dependent on the other; they are mutually strengthening.

There are risks involved in all love, acceptance and trust. If I come to understand another's inner world, if I can sense her confusion or his timidity or her feelings of being treated unfairly or his outrage at being ignored, if I can feel it as if it were my own, then a highly sensitive empathy comes into play between us. A rare kind of trusting-understanding develops. This is far different than the understanding that says: "I know what's wrong with you" or "I can see what makes you act that way."

This trusting-understanding enters the other's world in his or her own terms. And that is risky. If I take your world into mine, I run the risk of being changed, of becoming more like you.[6]

"You don't trust us anymore," your sons say as you refuse them the car and cancel their plans for a weekend at the beach. They're right. Your trust in them is at an all-time low, but you didn't want to hear it put so baldly. The risks of camping out on the dunes with all the other kids that wander into the state park in the spring are too much for you.

"Trust is not carte blanche," you say to yourself. "It has its limits. If the guys want trust, after the smashed fender, it would help if they would prove themselves for the next month." But you know from experience that demanding that trust be earned usually ends in mutual distrust and secrecy.

"I could say, 'Fellows, you want us to trust you to use your best judgment. Okay, we will. And it goes two ways. We want you to trust us to use our best judgment in setting a few limits . . .' "

How much are you willing to risk with them? What about a compromise that would risk halfway?

"What if I gave you the keys for a day at the beach, but no camping out? Back by midnight? What do you say?"

(Memo to self: It's possible to affirm trust in your sons even while limiting risks that have led to untrustworthy acts in the past. Risking what seems fair, safe, workable might rebuild faith.)

"I can't trust you anymore," parents sometimes say. The word "can't" is questionable. "I won't trust you anymore" might be a more honest statement. But the phrase has many meanings—

it may be about failed risk, about betrayed faith, about dashed hopes, about broken dreams; and it may be about the self—the parents' feelings of inadequacy, of fumbled permissiveness, of unadmitted neglect, of past failures of their own that lie unresolved. Beginning again with faith and risk, more risk and faith can then move both forward.

"You don't trust me anymore," children more often say to their parents. That's a line with many meanings.

It may be saying: "I'm confused. I've just betrayed my own ideals. I've done things I'm ashamed of. I know better. I've learned what does not work. I want to try again. Tell me that you trust me. I need a breath of trust."

Or it may be saying: "I'm angry. You talk about responsibility, but when I want to make a decision, you insist on making it for me. I need room to move, to breathe, to be me. Give me some elbow room."

Or it can mean: "I'm frustrated. You use your trust to manipulate me. I feel that your trust has many strings attached like, 'I'll trust you if . . . and only if . . .' But do you trust my ability to choose what seems right to me?"

Or it may mean: "I'm betrayed. You told me you trusted me, so I made the decision that seemed important to me. Now I see that you don't respect me or my decision at all. You set me up. You bear-trapped me. You led me to think I was free to choose, then snap! I'm caught and rejected."

Or the phrase may communicate: "I'm guilty. I let you down. I admit it. I need my quota of mistakes. If you expect me to be perfect—according to your stated standards—then 'trust' is the wrong word for our relationship. 'Obey' maybe, or 'copy.' But is that what you want—a rerun of your life?"

You stare at your silent son in total exasperation. "So you don't want to be a doctor or teach. But isn't there some respectable occupation that appeals to you?"

"Not what you're thinking about," he says. "I'm choosing to take a time out, rethink what I believe and want of life. Then maybe I'll find a little primitive land up north somewhere, with a simple house, and go back to the soil. I'd rather leave a smaller carbon footprint on the universe than we each do living in the suburbs and commuting to work in a cloud of smog. I know that doesn't fit with your dreams of my future. I don't share them anymore. I thought I did, all through study for my bachelor's degree. But now things don't look the same to me. Working and slaving for 40 years in the establishment only earns you ulcers and a taste for tranquilizers. Who needs all that capital at the cost of all those carbon emissions to be happy? Who needs all that worry about Dow Jones closings? I want to live."

You hear his values. They're worlds apart from your own. But they are out of concern for the world you share. Will you respect them? Or try to force him into some position where he has to yield to your values?

"Son," you could say, "I want to be able to appreciate your values whether I share them or not; and I want to know that you can see and respect my values too, even though you disagree with them." But you know that you are part of the problem in this polluted world, as he sees it, and you've spent your life working for a company that has profited by not dealing with it's role as a gross polluter.

"So it's a whole new playing field between us. Let's not let anything rain out the game. I want to be a part of your life, even if it leads you in an utterly different path from the one I have followed."

"Well, we could talk more. And read some of the same books. And debate whether you should quit your job and tell what you know about the ethics of sulfur production and its impact on the atmosphere."

You feel a surge of defensiveness, then decide to risk. "You've got a deal."

(Memo to self: If you lose trust with those you love most, what have you? Trust, risk, faith in each other, it's all we have.)

FOR FURTHER EXPERIENCE

Trust is an attitude that, although not observable, can be inferred from certain actions we call "trust-behaviors." Check yourself. Which behaviors are characteristic of **your** relationships?

Distrust	Trust
Constantly evaluating others.	Avoiding all value judgments of persons and personalities.
Directing judgmental statements at persons and personalities.	Objecting to specific behaviors, not the "behaver."
Attempting to control another's actions, words, expression of feelings.	Respecting freedom to think, feel, choose.
Using strategies to get desired outcomes, manipulation or threat.	Making simple, honest statements and clear open requests.
Acting neutral when feelings get tense.	Being willing to give of yourself when there is risk.
Acting distant and superior when another feels weak or hurt.	Being vulnerable as an equal with equals.
Demanding absolute promises and ironclad guarantees from others.	Allowing room for spontaneous choices, responses and actions.
Dogmatically asserting your opinions and viewpoints as right and always right.	Giving tentative statements that are open to others' feelings.

I blame you . . .
. . . and you blame me?

It's all your fault . . .
. . . it started with me?

It's your move first . . .
. . . it's all up to me?

Let's . . . call off the game.

"Love has good manners and does not pursue selfish advantage. It is not touchy. It does not keep account of evil or gloat over the wickedness of other people."

St. Paul, Letter of First Corinthians (13:5-6, *Phillips*)

6

ENDING BLAME:

Forget Whose Fault

I am writing this chapter in a public library. Suddenly the silence is split by the shrill ring of a cell phone, followed by a loud voice answering, shouting as though the phone will only work if the user replies in full voice. The conversation, not quickly terminated in deference to her location, goes on and on. Finally, someone gestures her toward the exit. The woman goes to stand by the exit but continues the conversation without lowering her voice a decibel. The whole library room of readers and students, interrupted and annoyed, are forced to listen to one-half of a tedious exchange. Finally, she ends the call, returns to the center of the room and announces in the same loud voice, "I'm sorry. That was rude, I know. I told them not to call me here, so it is their fault, not mine." Then, blame established, present company excepted (they, not I, were at fault), she smiles, having forgiven herself (forgiveness, the gift we give ourselves in a narcissistic age) and claims her books and chair.

Credo for chronic conflict: We must begin by figuring out and fingering the one who is to blame; it is not over until we have decided who is at fault. The content of the fight is not what matters. What matters is who started it, who is at fault, who should be blamed.

Motto for care-fronting conflict: You are always responsible for whatever you think, feel or do; I have no interest in blame.

You are always accountable for whatever you choose or do not choose; I do not wish to shame.

Responsibility is a concern in working through conflict. Defining who initiates the action, who owns the issues, who sets the boundaries are all part of responsibility, as is who takes the consequences and who stands to gain. But responsibility has a shadow side. No sooner is the word heard than it casts the punitive shadow called blame. This blame-shadow of responsibility impugns motives, demeans the self-worth of the person, punishes the actor for the bad action.

Effective confrontation is sharply focused on responsibility, expressed responsibly, addressed to responsibility.

Confrontation that places blame contains within itself the source of its own dysfunction. Blame inevitably evokes resistance and resentment, whether conscious at the moment or later upon reflection and review.

Confrontation that probes for shame possesses within itself the guarantee of its own defeat. Shame invariably elicits self-doubt and depressive pain, which then provoke new drives for expressing the original behavior again. The confrontation serves only to increase the actions it intended to eliminate.

Confrontation that stimulates responsibility invites the other person to look at past behavior more objectively and to consider new behavior that can be more satisfying to both persons. Such feedback simply recognizes the time boundaries that exist. The past must be honored as past, the present seized, the future envisioned.

Responsibility is focused on the present and its openness to the future. Responsibility recognizes the ability to respond, which is actual now and potential for what lies ahead: I will have ability to respond in the future; I have no ability to respond in the past. The past, being past, is not subject to change. I can change my present stance toward it and alter my future behavior from what I did in the past. These are present and future response-abilities.

Blame puts down the past as though that will help lift up better future options. (Instead, negative judgments and punitive actions toward one's past tend to boomerang. The negatively loaded behavior sticks in the memory and, in times of frustration, surfaces insistently.)

Shame puts down the self that acted in the past as though self-negations will create a positive self-image in the future. Two negations guarantee nothing except more negation.

Blame is powerless to effect change and growth. Shame is powerless to evoke inner direction and new course corrections.

But the capacity to choose creatively is increased as one takes responsibility for the past and affirms the ability to respond anew.

"I never liked that car—we shouldn't have bought it in the first place," your wife tells you. You're standing in the kitchen silently, accusingly, holding the crumpled chrome strip you just pulled loose from the smashed fender.

"It's just the fender," she says. "I scratched it."

"Scratched it? Who did you hit? Did you get a ticket? Does he have insurance?"

"Slow down. It was nothing like that. I scraped a post coming out of the parking lot. No accident. No police. No problem."

"Except for our $300 deductible insurance."

"Three-hundred-dollar what?"

"Never mind. Where were you looking?"

"Straight ahead. We shouldn't have bought that car to begin with. It's too low, you can't see out the other side. You paid too much. You were so in love with it."

"That's got nothing to do with this fender." You toss the chrome strip onto her white tablecloth. "We're talking about you trying to move a concrete abutment with a Corvette."

"You should be happy I wasn't hurt," she says. "If I had been run over by a truck, you'd come into the hospital and throw a filthy fender on my bed."

"Oh, for crying out loud, will you stick to the problem?"

"I am talking about the problem," she says. "It's always about who's to blame."

"The problem is I've got to pay for a smashed fender."

"The problem is not a piece of metal or money; it's us."

Nothing ends blaming games like the recognition that the blame, if properly scored, is most often 50-50.

Nothing settles old scores like the recognition that everything finally comes out even. That's how it is in any ongoing relationship. If there is blame to be fixed, it includes both persons involved.

It takes two people to have a problem. In a marriage, for example, neither I nor you is the whole problem. "We" are our problem. The trouble is with "us."

Both people are involved in the hurt, the problem, the tragedy of a marriage in pain.

Blame is 50-50. In marriage, both people deserve each other. All tends to come out even in the end.

Example one: "He's the problem," the wife says. "I've given him the best 20 years of my life. I've cared for him in sickness and in health; I've borne him three children; I've never refused him anything. Now look. He betrays me with some little tramp. See how I was wronged?"

Good speech. Good case for scoring blame 90-10. Ninety for him—the villain; 10 for her—the virtuous wife. Agreed?

Highly unlikely. When you've heard them both, things even out. Once you see how righteous and superior she appears to him, the score comes nearer to 50-50 again.

Example two: "It's all her fault that our son ran away," a husband says. "She nagged at him mercilessly. She criticized his choice of friends. She picked at his hair, his clothes, his way of speaking. She refused to accept the girl he was dating. So the boy left. She drove him away."

He makes a good case for scoring the tragedy 99-1. Ninety-nine points against her; one for his own responsibility.

But when you've heard both sides, the points even out. In this case, the dad kept his distance from his wife since the boy was quite young. His cool withdrawal taught the boy how to reject and write his mother off. So the boy did in reality what his dad has been doing all along—withdrawing, rejecting, running away from relationship and intimacy.

Whose fault is it when things go wrong? That's the first question that arises in many human difficult moments. For those who prefer placing responsibility elsewhere, the question leads to a wild chase for the goat, we say, the scapegoat who gets the blame. For those who prefer to sponge up the anger and store it away inside, the blame can be taken heroically upon themselves. "It's all my fault," they say. "I'm the total failure." And even more people do both. At one moment they blame themselves for the whole tragedy; at the next moment they take another swing at the scapegoat.

Blaming ourselves is useless for a variety of reasons.

We usually blame ourselves for all the wrong reasons. (The crucial things that went wrong are not likely to occur to us alone.)

We're not qualified to sit in final judgment of our own lives. We so easily slip into total rejection, "I'm no good at all, I don't deserve to live," or we excuse ourselves lightly, "So what? I'm only human." (To assume the right to sit in judgment over my motives, my past and my true condition, is to play God.)

If the blamer within wins, both sides lose. The blamer and the blamed are both on the wrong side—the side of self-punishment that rarely leads to new beginnings, the side of self-negation that critiques the past. But those things that one resents and resists are the things one most often repeats. We change not by trying to condemn who we are or were, but as we accept ourselves—our pasts—as the truth about our struggles and stop self-abuse of our failures, and look in new directions. Self-criticism tends to be cyclical, trying the same thing over and over, repeating the same efforts and attempts. We need new insight into our history that comes when we stop attacking and start listening carefully to what is going on in our lives. None of us truly understands our past. Our memories are selective. We recall those things that fit with our self-image.

Friedrich Nietzsche, the German philosopher, put this pointedly, saying, "Pride and memory had an argument. Memory said, 'It happened thus and so!' Pride replied, 'Oh, but it couldn't have been like that!' and memory gave in."[7]

So it is for us all. Memory gives in again and again. Most of the pictures we recall from our past have been retouched. Most of the scripts we can quote from old conversations have been edited for us by pride.

Memory is *museum.*

Room on room of memories are instantly available as one flashes through collections of choice recollections at will. Musing through your museum, note how selective the artifacts are. Are they art or fact? Did you create them to meet your needs or capture them to record reality?

Memory is *mystery.*

"I can see it now exactly as it happened," you may insist. But it isn't true. The best you can do is produce a biased series of fragments that serve to reassure you that things were as you wish they were. Or they may warn you to be sure they do not recur. The truth of your past is known only in part. Even to you—especially to you.

Memory is *myth.*

Some people believe that memory is a camera. They assume that past events are accurately recorded through an objective lens and preserved without being retouched. We have no objective past. Our reflections are just that. My memories mirror me and my needs, my values, my dreams, my interpretation of my serial life experiences. Memory is not a telescope for looking at a sharply etched and permanent image. Memory is a kaleidoscope that reviews the past, rearranges its detail, reinterprets its meanings for the challenges of the moment. My story is my mythology of my life, which guides the organization of my life. Memory is a compass that may repaint the scenes recalled but still points toward integrity. Memory is a gyroscope that balances the self and maintains harmony and unity within.

Memory is *my story*.

Myth or mystery, it's still my story, and it's a story worth telling. Yes, it has been thoroughly edited by my pride. Memory reports what took place and pride rewrites the data before the conscience—the perfect scribe—can get at it. Yes, it has been recycled, and the most recent forms may be made up of the original atoms, but the anatomy has matured. Still, it's my story of who I am today, what I am becoming now, where I stand in this moment.

"Museum tours daily, 9:00 to 5:00."

Venture into your museum. Claim the rooms. The treasure is yours. Explore. The valuables are precious property. They are evidence that you have lived, risked, failed, learned from the pain, grown, celebrated, broken free.

There are a few rules in the museum.

Appreciate the collected objects of art. Don't abuse the privilege of visiting your past. Do not vandalize your valuables. Look at them in appropriate awe. Do not criticize them. Prize them.

Respect the recollected experiences. Use them for you, not against you. Learn from them how to choose more freely, how to live more fully, how to act more faithfully in the future.

Acquit the memories from any and all charges. To attempt to change the unchangeable (what is done is done) is useless. To try to reform what is formed (what was, is) is pointless.

Be humble enough to take pride in your past. Great or small, it's yours. Have the grace to be grateful for having lived. Accept the grace to own how you have lived. Absorb the grace that frees you to delight in what you have lived.

Going through our old memories to place blame is like hunting for a black bead in a dark room at midnight, wearing heavy gloves and a blindfold.

Rather, I want to own my past with as few defenses as possible and live now in the present before God and with my brothers and sisters.

Recognizing how unable I am to judge myself brings me to awareness of how unqualified I am to judge a sister or a brother. Since my vision is as impaired as though a beam of wood were protruding from my eye, I am poorly equipped to remove splinters from others, as Jesus unforgettably taught us.

Pass no judgment,
And you will not be judged.
For as you judge others,
So you will yourselves be judged,
And whatever measure you deal out to others
Will be dealt back to you.
Why do you look at the speck of sawdust in your
  brother's eye,
With never a thought for the great plank in your own?
Or how can you say to your brother,
"Let me take the speck out of your eye,"
When all the time there is that plank in your own?
You hypocrite!
First take the plank out of your own eye,

And then you will see clearly
To take the speck out of your brother's.
Matthew 7:1-5, *NEB*

Paul put it this way:

Love keeps no score of wrongs;
Does not gloat over other men's sins,
But delights in the truth.
There is nothing love cannot face;
There is no limit to its faith, its hope,
and its endurance.
1 Corinthians 13:5-7, *NEB*

Love ends the blaming games and gets on to the real questions: What is the loving, responsible, truly respectful thing to do now? Where do we go from here? When do we start? If not from here—where? If not now—when? Who—if not you and me?

Loving means owning responsibility, breaking the lead from the fine-line bookkeeping pencil, tearing up the scorecard and beginning again. *Now.*

FOR FURTHER EXPERIENCE

1. Discuss a sensitive difference between you and a second party—family member, husband, wife, colleague—after covenanting the following ground rules:

   (1) All language must be in present tense.

   (2) All comments must be here and now.

   (3) All statements must begin with "I feel . . ." (and give real feelings, not "I feel *that* . . ." which is a judgment, idea or criticism masquerading in a feeling language).

   (4) All blame statements are discarded as soon as either recognizes the finger being pointed.

Now move on up to an even more sensitive beef (or complaint). See if you can maintain clear, simple, feeling-wanting statements.

2. Finish the following sentences for each other with at least three endings:

   "I appreciate . . ."

   "I want . . ."

   "I need . . ."

   "I demand . . ."

   "I resent . . ."

Hear each other. Cancel old hidden demands. Drop blaming strategies and work toward what you truly want for yourself, for each other, for you both together.

Order.
Please rise.
The honorable
Everyman presiding.
You may be seated.
Case one.
Humanity vs. you.
How do you plead?
Guilty or not guilty?

"No condemnation
now hangs over the head of those who are 'in' Christ Jesus."

St. Paul, Letter to Romans (8:1-2, *Phillips*)

7

CASE DISMISSED:

Reclaiming the Gavel

"What will people think?" you ask your daughter. "What will people say? That kind of thing just isn't done around here. I don't want to hear any more about it."

You see frustration turning to anger in your daughter's eyes. She's up against the old wall "what will people think?"

You hated that wall when your parents pointed to it; now you are using it to shut in your daughter. Must you truly first consider, "How will it look to others? What will it do to our family name?" How you feel or what you believe matters little when the final choice hangs on others' values.

"Is that what I want for my daughter?" you ask yourself. "Blind obedience to others' expectations? What has it done for me?"

"Maybe it matters less than I think. Why am I always on trial? Always afraid of what people will say? I should hear her idea again. I doubt if I was really listening."

(Memo to self: If I am only an echo, what am I?)

It is extremely difficult to be civil with others when one is engaged in a civil war within the self. It is very hard to hear others when one has blocked out the voices from within one's own soul. It is virtually impossible to be nonjudgmental when one is constantly on trial before an inner judge or before a world of accusing judges that are constantly reviewing your case. When one is consistently on trial, either feeling judged or acting as judge, all communication is contaminated by this imaginary game of legal charades.

As long as you are on trial before others, or sit in judgment over others in your inner courtroom, your relationships are vertical—talking down to others or talking up to others. Effective communication is level—single level, talking with others in give and take. Clear communication and clean confrontation that create good dialogue with others occurs when we speak as equals. No "judgment" intended. No "judgment received." Good judgment expressed and evoked in us both.

Open communication can be received with little distortion as one vacates the "hot seat" and is no longer on trial for what he or she does, fails to do or is. Confrontation can be clearly heard when one is no longer feeling automatically charged or guilty as charged.

"Wake up," your conscience commands. "It's time to be in court."

"Right, your honor," you reply. Another day in court has begun.

Your conscience sits as judge at the foot of the bed. As you shave, and brush and floss, you will undergo questioning. Once downstairs, your mother, dad, husband, wife, will join in or take the conscience's elevated place at the bench. Then, at work, the boss will pick up the gavel. At lunch, Charlie will preside while you tell him about last night's problem with the neighbor who backed over your bike. Tonight at home your brother-in-law Pete ("They're coming over for supper, remember?") will be presiding.

And what's in it for you? A long-running trial. You're in the docket, permanently. One judge follows another. The evidence is heard. You testify—often against yourself. Sentence is passed—"guilty" (it's an extremely rare occasion that you receive "not guilty"). Most often your case is passed on to the next judge.

Life is a courtroom. All around you a jury is seated. Someone holds the gavel. You take the stand. Some days, in classic form, you choose "in the stocks," or in extreme situations, you fear the gallows and feel the noose around your neck.

You know the feeling—the feeling of being constantly on trial? That life is not a stage but a courtroom? That others have been appointed to judge? And you? You're the judged. Always on trial.

You are constantly making judicial appointments. You are handing out robes and gavels. You are constantly on trial because you place yourself on trial. Every day is your day in court. Every man is your judge. Every disapproval is a new ruling, another sentence.

"Claiming love for yourself is the real secret," Dr. Frank Kimper counsels. "There was a time when—though I was loved, I did not have the courage to claim it. Depressed, lonely, I felt no one cared about me. It wasn't really true, but I lived as though it were; and as a result, I was sick at heart and sick in body. I worked for praise, thinking that love had to be earned. I assumed that to be praised was to be loved, and to be criticized was to be rejected. So I was always on trial."[8]

Few things are more painful than to be always on trial, constantly working for praise. Praise is a ruling in your favor. Enough praise might add up to an acquittal. But it is highly unlikely that there will ever be enough praise to convince you that you're okay.

"To be praised is to be loved" is the secret message you unconsciously tell yourself. It was true, of course, when you were a child in the concrete thinking period before age seven; but no longer. To be praised more often is to be manipulated. To be praised is often to be used. To be praised is often to be outsmarted, outmaneuvered, out-sweet-talked. But when you live to be praised, it doesn't matter. No price is too great for a little praise. "Can't get enough of that praise!"

But when you get it, it turns to vapor in your grasp. You work for praise and approval, live for commendations and compliments, even sacrifice just for recognition and public notice. And what do you have to show for it? Emptiness. Loneliness. And little of the love you wanted so much.

Why? Because there is another side that seems to haunt you. Criticism. And to be criticized is to be rejected. To be criticized is to lose approval, respect, love and everything you're working toward. That's not true either, of course. To be criticized is often to be truly appreciated. To be respected so much that the other person can share both positive and negative feelings about you. To be criticized by a real friend can be a form of love.

But when you put yourself on trial, criticism is seen as rejection, and praise is viewed as acceptance. What a way to live! What a way to *not* live. To be constantly on trial is not living. It is existing as a shadow, a reflection of others' approval or disapproval. It can all end whenever you want it to. No one is constantly on trial unless she or he chooses to be. If you live for another's praise or cringe rejected under another's criticism, you are choosing to be on trial. You volunteer to be victim; you give others far too much power.

You are you. Claim yourself for who you are as a person of worth. Own yourself as a person with dignity. Reclaim the power to be who you are in spite of your moment-to-moment performance, regardless of your day-to-day achievements. Be who you are before God and before others.

When you are permanently off trial, when your judges have been reclaimed as friends, equals, colleagues, then you will notice that a key difference begins to occur in most of your relationships. You no longer wield a gavel over others. When you are off trial, your friends, enemies, coworkers will be acquitted as well.

Reclaiming the gavels once distributed and refusing the gavels others delegate to you are two sides of the same process of ending a long search for exorbitant approval and validation. The need to be validated by one's peers continues lifelong as a desirable and confirming exchange of appreciation and approval. But exaggerating the need for the confirmation of those about you until it resounds with the rap of the gavel, or is rated with the flash of scorecards (9.8, 9.8, 9.8, whoops, 5.2!). When the locus of evaluation for one's life is external in the eyes and nods of others, one has no center. As the locus of evaluation, decision and life direction is internalized, one becomes a responsible agent, a mature person, a fully functioning adult. Gavels are to be collected and discarded; if the other refuses to give your gavel back, it is no longer yours, it is theirs, and they are responsible for its use. You may then ignore it. If another has entrusted you with gavel power over them, refuse the privilege.

A second son said to his older brother, "I have a strange request to make. For years I have given you a gavel to pass judgment on me—on my work, on my marriage, on matters of taste—the list of issues that I looked to you for approval or feared your judgment is long. I have no idea if you understood the role I cast you in. It doesn't matter. I gave you a bushel of gavels, one for every issue or area of concern. I am asking for them all back. I want to be your brother, not a defendant pleading my case before you." *(Memo to self: Get back every gavel.)*

An older sister said to her younger sister, "I don't know what has gotten into you; you used to value my opinion. Now you no longer take my point of view with the same seriousness as before. I'm upset that you are not measuring up to what you should be." *(Memo to self by younger sister: Now that my gavels are no longer available, you are using your own.)*

A second son said to his older brother, "I was so intimidated by your perfection, so frustrated working with—no, under—you. I spent years trying to measure up to your standard, to fulfill your expectations. I finally had to get away. I knew no other way to escape feeling constantly judged. So I asked for an advance of my inheritance, and I left home. I took you with me in my gut, and I spent the money to spite your frugal example. I partied with strangers to scandalize your demands for being upright and straight-laced. Now I am broke, and I've been trying to survive by feeding pigs. At wit's end, I've come home, and our father welcomed me back, embraced and forgave me. Here I am—new robe, shoes, ring of authority. I'm back in the family. But you have not spoken to me. If I do not recognize your right to be my judge, who will you be to me? If I am not willing to return to being constantly on trial before you, how can I relate to you? (Compare Luke 15:11-31.)

Think of those persons whose approval is all-important to you. Visualize them. Fantasize them seated behind a bench, gavel in hand, powdered wig in place. Do you see their approving or judging faces? Now—in your mind—go to each one of them. Say, "I have given you the power to try me, to sentence me, to reject me. When you reject me, I reject myself. When you approve of me, I approve of myself. My happiness, wellbeing and self-respect depend on your approval."

It sounds so powerless, so spineless to actually say those things aloud, doesn't it? But go ahead. Try it out. If you do not find that the image fits, you can discard it. Say to that face who is now frowning at you, "I reclaim my responsibility for me. I am no longer giving you the power to reject me and cut me off from love, joy and happiness. I am re-owning myself."

Now you're facing the real issue. Will you accept love from others without needing first to pay in advance? Without needing first to earn it, then to receive it? Will you claim love for yourself? Will you bear to be loved whether you feel you deserve it or not?

We're at a very crucial point here. *Accepting love*. For many it's unpalatable. Unacceptable. Love is only to be accepted in return for work well done. I've been there myself. Even when I was told I was loved whether my performance matched all expectations or not, I didn't believe it. I explained it away. When others affirmed me as someone who is loved, I rationalized it away. It only made matters worse to be loved.

Until I received it gratefully. Claimed and accepted it. No questions asked.

That is what the New Testament calls "grace." To be loved—and to need to accept that love—right at the point where we don't deserve it. As the text says, in loose translation, "But God, rich in mercy, for the great love He bore us, and the immense resources of His grace, and great kindness to us in Christ Jesus, made us His own. By His affection unearned you are forgiven. It is not your own doing. It is God's gift, not a reward for work done. There is nothing for anyone to boast of" (see Eph. 2:4-10).

As the announcement of trial adjourned is heard, somewhere deep in the soul a fearful voice may ask, "You mean that I'm not on trial?" ("Only if you put yourself on the block.") "And I needn't fear you as my judge?" ("I don't want the job. Reclaim your power to be you. Affirm your freedom to be yourself. Your trial is over.")

In the concrete thought of early childhood, the link between performance and acceptance is not dissolvable, but we tell the child the good news anyway.

I like you as you are,
Exactly and precisely.
I think you turned out nicely.[9]

This song lyric by the late Reverend Fred Rogers, a favorite of the little people who watched his award-winning children's TV program *Mister Rogers' Neighborhood,* is a celebration of unearned love. A child can absorb such love long before he or she is capable of understanding that it is given without regard for appearance, compliance or performance.

For an adult, to accept acceptance when we know that we are unacceptable is, for many, an unbearable, impossible task. To receive help and admit that we cannot help ourselves is no easy thing. For many it's an unpalatable thing they simply will not endure. So they must stay stuck with their feelings of rejection, hung up with the need to pay their own way, frozen at the one point of great opportunity.

To accept another's acceptance at the moment you see yourself as unacceptable, this is grace. And grace received is experienced as joy.

To give joy to another is to extend grace—love without conditions and limitations—to another. It is to admire, appreciate and enjoy another without trying to change him or her by rejecting parts of that person as unacceptable or intolerable.

To enjoy another is like enjoying a sunset. You do not command, "Tone down the reds. Raise the lavenders. Stop! Too much yellow. A bit more blue, please." You are not in command. You are in awe. You view it with respect and appreciation. To see another person unfold and to enjoy that unfolding—that is grace.

Joy happens when we can truly accept another—and are accepted. "What if I am unacceptable? What if I am rejected?" we wonder in fear. And at the moment when rejection is expected, acceptance is discovered in the other's smile.

Joy is the result of truly loving and being loved by another—warts, faults, quirks and all. Have you not experienced it when a friend comes close enough to see faults and blemishes, as well as virtues and strengths, and still loves you? "He knows what I'm really like. She knows me for what I truly am. Yet I am loved."

Joy happens when we can truly hear another and be truly heard. Have you not experienced joy when a friend shows caring in the only believable way—by hearing not just your words, but hearing you? And your heart wants to shout, "I've been heard. Someone else knows what it's like to be me." You feel it in the chest and around the eyes. It's a moistness. Like tears. Tears of joy. Joy is the enjoyment of being enjoyed, in a parallel way to the way grace is the acceptance of being accepted. And love is seeing another as precious, just as you know yourself to be precious.

When you're driving alone, and the hours stretch long, you may find yourself in long conversations with your soul, talking to yourself, answering yourself and then listening in surprise to your own wisdom.

When talking out loud in the monologue called prayer, some things are said that can only be said to God—the deepest feeling, searching, longing for what is valued above all else. Try it often, when you are alone.

When the feelings and thoughts are all out, experience what follows—the silence, the openness, the release. Then listen. You may now be in touch with what you've really been wanting, to truly know that you are loved. Accept the truth; you are accepted.

FOR FURTHER EXPERIENCE

1. Do you tend to feel judged and condemned when you hear how others see you, what they expect of you and where they differ or disapprove? Go to that person in your imagination and say, "I hear your expectations. I am not responsible for them. I want to be who I am and still be in relationship with you. I am responsible for that."

2. Affirm to yourself: "When I have chosen to act according to my values . . .

   (1) "I will not reject or regret my action merely because someone has passed judgment or volunteered criticism against it.

   (2) "I will not disown, deny or feel a need to make excuses or justify my behavior.

   (3) "I will change my ways of behaving out of respect for others' feelings and rights, or because I am finding more satisfying ways of relating to others—but not out of fear of their judgment or censure."

3. Say these affirmations to someone you love:

   (1) "I am equally precious, as you are precious. Our abilities may differ; our worth, never."

   (2) "I no longer question my worth as a person, even when I feel that others may."

   (3) "When you criticize me, I will see you as caring and confronting me. I want to hear the criticism and not

feel attacked or rejected. When you praise me, I will say a simple 'Thank you.' "

When things are going well,
I say, "Don't change."
When things are getting tense,
I say, "You change."
When you get angry,
I say, "I'll change."
When things are going rough,
I say, "You'll never change."
When you do change,
I say, "Change back."

"I forget all that lies behind me and with hands outstretched to whatever lies ahead I go straight for the goal."

St. Paul, Letter to Philippians (3:13-14, *Phillips*)

8

GETTING UNSTUCK:

Experiencing the Freedom to Change

A police car pulls up under the streetlight in front of the town hall-police station combination in a small Midwestern town. Two deputies pull a disheveled girl from the back seat. She flinches under their rough handling.

A crowd of men follow them into the office of the justice of the peace.

"We caught this hippie slut sleeping in a haystack with two long-haired apes. They got away. But she's gonna get it for all three of 'em."

"Whatta we do to her?" someone asks.

"Wait'll the J. P. gets here; we'll find out."

"The little tramp. She oughta be horsewhipped to an inch of her life. That useta be the law around here."

A man pushes through the crowd. He kneels beside the terrified, weeping girl.

"Have a little pity," he says gently, looking up at the hard, leering circle of faces.

"Okay, stranger," a deputy demands, "what do you say we do to her? We caught her in the hay with a couple of horny hippies. Don't you think she oughta have it beaten out of her?"

The man straightens up. "The one of you who is without fault, let him strike the first blow," he says evenly, looking from face to face.

An old man is first to leave. Then another. And others. The room empties. Only the man remains with the girl, still lying on the floor, sobbing.

"Where are all your accusers?" the man asks. "Has no one struck you?"

"No, no one," she replies.

"I don't condemn you either," he says gently. "You may go. You're not stuck to the old script. You're free to live a new way. You don't need to repeat all this again." (Compare John 8:1-11.)

Some personalities seem virtually incapable of change. Their behavior viewed over years of cyclical repetition of the same self-defeating patterns might lead an observer to conclude that change among humans occurs rarely and slowly if at all.

Other personalities make great strides in growth, develop unrecognized gifts, learn new ways of being in relationships. What makes this striking difference?

Not all humans possess the same potential for change— the same malleability, adaptability, flexibility, resilience. There is significant variation in the capacities to turn toward new goals, focus on new alternatives and commit oneself in new directions.

Basing their judgment on those who resist and inhibit change, some conclude that people are largely the product of their past; that persons are the direct consequences of their early childhood development; that humans are basically conditioned by their social situation. They see limited possibility in education or in any confrontation because minimal change, growth, adaptation are to be expected from the adult human. "You can't change human nature!" they often quote.

Others, in contrast, look at those persons who are open to the invitations given by friends, educators, counselors, pastors and respond with astounding courage and creativity to claim new ways of relating, redirecting and realizing new sides of the self. As a result, observers who focus on such persons who delight in growth tend to see humans as the creatures that possess the gift of changing, growing, creating and recreating behaviors. From this perspective to learn is to change; to learn is to grow; to learn is to become more than and different from what and who one has been.

Learning is integrative, not additive, so all real learning involves a change of one's core self. Learning reorganizes the mass of information we carry within us and allows us to reconfigure attitudes and assumptions in new ways. Change, and the ability to continue adventuring in the change process, is at the center of our humanness, our aliveness, our uniqueness as children of God. The man in the story that opened this chapter was such a change agent. His first word in His teaching was "Change!"

To say that change is improbable or impossible, to say, "I can't change," is to secretly suspect that my life is controlled by fate. The script for such a lifestyle goes something like this:

I had no voice in my birth.
I had no choice of parents,
I had no alternatives to my family,
I am the product of my environment,
Conditioned by the controls of my community.
By the time I was five,
My personality was set.
I grew up in a vise.
I could barely breathe, move, risk.
I had no say about anything.
I had to stay in line,
No back talk, no negotiation.
By the time I was a teenager,
I had become who I am.
I never had much of a chance.
Not enough love, support, trust, faith.
Not the parenting, training,
Not the models for maturing.

Not a good education,
No real choice of vocation.
Not one chance to change it.
Not a single opportunity to be different.
It's all in the stars/cards/genes
In the fates/script/conditioning.
They determined who I am.
I had all the wrong breaks, no luck.
I'll die when my number comes up,
And that's that.
I've little or no choice.
I can't help it.

The first two are true. You did not choose to be born, nor did you select your parents; but from there on, it is a list of falsehoods. You are not passive; you become a participant. You possess the capacity to think in new ways, to see from other perspectives, dream other dreams and move in new directions.

And your relationships are open, not closed, to change. You may have learned that conformity is safe and individuality is dangerous, but you are free to test that assumption again. You may have been taught that silent withdrawal is better than getting involved in working out relationships, but you are not stuck with that strategy forever. You may have seen models of stubborn authoritarian ways of being right, but you do not have to go through life insisting on your own way. You have the freedom to be flexible if you are willing to risk; the freedom to negotiate if you decide for mutual relating with others.

There, we have just reviewed the core set of conflict styles that seem so hard to change, but they are not that difficult to challenge in oneself. What is needed is a good model—seeing someone "care and confront" in balanced genuineness—and the willingness to experiment in replicating it in one of your relationships. This experiment in re-envisioning your ways of responding to others is not that difficult. It means saying, "Let me watch how you do that," "Yes, I see how that works," "I can do that."

Let's do such an experiment. Focus your mind on one of your friends—a friend whom you respect. Someone who has gifts you admire, convictions you envy and the courage to follow them. There. You have a face in mind. Now let's imagine what that person might make of your life in one day, if he or she were given the opportunity.

This is an exercise in creative imaging. If you allow yourself to explore it, there are intriguing discoveries awaiting you.

It's morning. You've just pasted your toothbrush and begun a vigorous brushing when you glance up at the mirror. It is not your familiar face that peers back, but the face of your friend. The toothbrush clatters into the basin. You stand, openmouthed in dazed unbelief. How often you've said, "I wish I were in his or her shoes for just one day, and he/she in mine. I'd like to see someone else face what I put up with every day."

Now it has happened. Somewhere, just now, another person may be staring at your face in his or her mirror, going downstairs to eat your breakfast, driving your car to your job, interacting with your friends, living today with the results of your decisions made in a thousand yesterdays.

One of the best persons you know has just moved into your life, into where it is, as it is. What changes will be made? Will a fresh viewpoint make a real difference? Will a new spirit of hope and optimism infect your job, your friends, your work? How will the abandonment of worn-out habits of thought and action change your routine acts and the responses of your associates? Can one day's practice of new behavior patterns make a significant difference in the world you normally touch?

What are the differences? Are they differences you want now? Changes you need now? What is stopping *you* from making those changes? How are you keeping yourself from being the different person that your work needs, your world needs, you need? How are you stopping yourself? You are stopping yourself from becoming all you can be.

You are free to change if you choose. Change as a person, change in your power-to-live, change in claiming your potentials.

"You didn't want me," the girl said to her mother. "You have never wanted me." For 14 years the girl has lived under the burden of a thoughtless word, an off-hand comment that to a child was a revelation.

"We weren't expecting twins, so the second one came as a great shock." The mother's comment, overheard by the little girl at play, was her earliest memory. Feeling unwanted, she withdrew. The mother, not understanding, left her to her loneliness.

Now that she's aware of the injury inflicted by her careless words, what's the mother to do? Punish herself for her lack of awareness? Hate herself for the damage done to a sensitive girl? Neither would be helpful to either.

She can *start over.* Start over by owning the responsibility for her part in neglecting and ignoring her daughter. "I am sorry you carried that thoughtless word all these years. It was wrong. I want you. I want to be close to you now." Begin again by acting responsibly now. She can plan new ways of being close, new times for listening and conversation, new ways of reaching out to say, "I care. Watch me. See how much I care."

Starting over has many names. "Take it from the top," we say. "Is there a second chance, a second try, a rematch, a new beginning?" Theologically it is called "repentance." Repentance is owning responsibility for what was, accepting responsibility for what is, and acting responsibly now. Repentance is responsible action. It is not a matter of punishing ourselves for past mistakes, hating ourselves for past failures and depressing ourselves with feelings of worthlessness. Repentance is becoming aware of where my responsibility begins and ends, and acting responsibly. Repentance is finishing the unfinished business of my past and choosing to live in new ways that will not repeat old, unsatisfactory situations.

"Somewhere along the way I missed it," a father says. He's standing in the doorway of his son's room, looking at the empty bed. It's 2:00 A.M. God knows where he is. Or what he's up to now. "I don't know how or where it started, but I blew it as a dad. I really blew it."

He stands, head against the doorframe, going back through the past 17 years, wishing he'd done the other thing, and hurting, for his son and for himself. This stewing in guilt over mistakes made in parenting lets guilt and anger build to the breaking point; then he takes it out on his son again.

He sat helpless while his sons were growing through their teenage years. "They won't obey me. There's nothing I can do. I'm a failure as a dad," he would say.

Meanwhile, the boys grew bitter at his lack of strength, his unwillingness to stand up to them, his softness when challenged.

Can he start over, or has he missed his chance? Is it too late?

"What if I told my son where I hurt instead of telling him what's wrong with him?" he might ask himself. "What if I told him that I care instead of cutting him down? I get in this cycle of—I feel guilty about my son—so I get angry at my son—so I feel guiltier and I get angrier. Admitting where I am could be at least a first step to freedom."

Starting over would require that this father own his responsibility for copping out on his sons, recognize how he is avoiding all confrontation with them and stand up alongside them. But does he care enough to risk confronting them with his own strength? (He has strength enough. He's been using most of it to protect himself.) He can love them enough to let them test their budding strength against his, prove their decision-making ability by matching it with his.

Starting over begins in owning responsibility for what has been, wasting no time in self-punishment or self-hate and getting on with the kind of behavioral changes that accept responsibility for initiating what can be. Whenever a man or a woman accepts responsibility for where she or he is (that's often called confession) and chooses to make a change (that's often called repentance) and reaches out for the strength of God and the accepting love of some significant other persons (that's often called conversion), then change begins.

It is the growing person who can honestly say, "I have done wrong. I own it. It was my action. I am responsible for it. I am choosing to end that way of behaving. I am choosing to live in a new way."

The capacity to *start over* is directly related to our willingness to see. You've got to see how it really is before you can truly take responsibility. It takes courage to see our relationships clearly as others see them. We are afraid, and rightly so. Usually we are afraid for the wrong reason.

We fear, "If I let myself see what really is, all will collapse." It is not so.

Our real fear should rather be that things will not collapse, that things will not change, that we're likely to repeat the same errors over and over again; that, unless we own our mistakes responsibly and take responsibility to change, we'll be stuck forever where we are now.

Starting over (repentance in the full Christian meaning of the word) is a process. It's a thawing out of rigid lifestyles into a flowing, moving, growing, repenting process. It is getting off the safe bank of isolation and into the flowing river of change and discovery and a growing life.

Starting over has two key concepts: vulnerability and responsibility. Both of these are processes. They continue as long as life continues.

A word on vulnerability.

Vulnerability is letting the need for change get through my defenses. If I need to admit to you that I make mistakes, I freeze. If I am about to be honest about my failures, my sudden fear is that I will lose your respect, your trust, perhaps your friendship. It's likely not true, of course, but my inner defenses keep telling me that it is so. Starting over begins in honest owning of my own fears. Voluntary vulnerability creates trust, makes respect possible and builds friendship. (This is not self-depreciation done either in self-hate or false humility, but simply owning my own experience for what it is.)

Vulnerability initiates, I discover, the most consistently beautiful and meaningful experiences in human relationships. People are lovable when vulnerable. People are believable when vulnerable. People come to life as real, living, breathing, hurting, feeling, laughing, singing, growing beings when they are vulnerable.

But the price is humility, not pride's protection; authenticity, not pretending. No person ever achieves safe-and-serene invulnerability. But we can pretend it. We can dream that it is possible, work to make it probable in our own lives and carry on as if we are carrying it off, but we never arrive. Our pronouncements continue to be questioned. Our pretenses are constantly suspect. Our claimed expertise is never beyond criticism. We are vulnerable. We feel it even as we deny it. We might as well affirm it. Might as well own our vulnerability. Vulnerability is letting humility replace my old defense strategies with simple honesty, simple openness, simple willingness to change and grow.

A word on responsibility.

Responsibility is letting hope awaken and turn my actions in new directions, toward more constructive actions. It is difficult to stop hearing the word "responsible" as a command, "You're responsible," a command made by some authority—either conscience within or some controlling force without. But the real meaning of the word is response-ability—the ability to respond.

Persons with responsibility are persons discovering the possibility to respond to others in free, vulnerable honesty.

You will find that as you choose to be vulnerable to others in admitting who you are, where you have failed, how you hurt and what you truly want in life, that the strength to respond in new ways—the response-ability—is there. Some of it is your own strength. Much more of it is the strength of God's Spirit within. (Who of us knows where the one ends and the other begins? We are only thankful that strength, courage, endurance and patience are there. These are the abilities to respond.)

Starting over—this pairing of open vulnerability with honest response-ability—is a continuous, ongoing process throughout life, a change-inspiring center of one's lifestyle. It's the key to growth, to relationship, to discovering God at work in transforming human experience through hope. Hope that change is possible. Hope that we can be forgiven, loved, accepted by both God and my co-travelers in life if we own who we are, what we've done and where we are going now. Hope that life can be new.

Yesterday, in a tense interchange, I hurt a friend with words that were too surgical. No matter what led up to it, I am responsible for the thoughtless words that cut. I have voiced my regret and my promise to not repeat such speech. I am choosing to relate to that person in a more gentle way in the future. This is starting over in repentance. I own responsibility for my part in what was unsatisfactory between us. I refuse to analyze and place blame for the other's part. I accept responsibility for my part in what is and what will be new behavior.

When Jesus came among us, His first words were, "Turn, change, start over, the kingdom of right relationships, the reign of God's justice, the new upside-down world of hope is here. Repent and believe the good news" (turn, change, believe that you are free to love and be loved, that you can act justly and truthfully, that you can live in a way that is truthful in a world that is false). As Phillips translates these words, "The time has come at last—the kingdom of God has arrived. You must change your hearts and minds and believe the good news" (Mark 1:15, *Phillips*).

Another way of naming how we get stuck is to observe those areas in which we have come to rely on stereotypes or think in trusted repetitive patterns recorded automatically from our cultures. Many of these are harmless forms of shorthand, but all too many are composed of negative judgments. Prejudice is any collection of negative feelings based on judgments that are not readily changed even in the face of data that challenges or disproves them. Prejudice is any set of negative valuations based upon an inflexible generalization. We stick to them; we get stuck with them.

The process of forming these generalizations called prejudices flows as follows:

We categorize to maintain our sanity. Grouping things, thoughts and people into classes is necessary in order to handle the complexity of our world. The trap lies in our tendency to exaggerate differences between groups on a particular characteristic and to minimize the differences within all groups.

We stereotype to maintain our equilibrium. It throws us off balance to constantly be observing differences, so we attribute certain traits to large human groups. Often these are images chosen to justify a negative feeling—fear, threat, inferiority. It is a head theory to support what the heart wants to make true.

We sanitize all incoming data to maintain purity of opinions. By being selective on what we expose ourselves to, we automatically limit our contacts and possibilities. By being selective with attention, we unconsciously exclude all incompatible data. By being selective in our recall, we drop out conflictual facts. So only supportive evidence is admitted and any contradiction is seen as an exception to the rule, which goes to prove the rule.

So we discriminate in feeling, then in thought process, then in action. And the contradictions go unnoticed.

For example, the traits considered a virtue in the groups we like (because we are like them) are seen as a vice when observed in members of unlike groups. If one is a white Anglo-Saxon Protestant, he or she will admire Lincoln for being thrifty, hardworking, eager to learn, ambitious, successful. In a Jew, such traits would be called stingy, miserly, driven, uncharitable, and so on.

Life changes from moment to moment. I, too, can change, unless I choose to be stuck with, or stick by, old, narrow, self-defeating ideas and ways of behaving. Healing can come as I become willing to risk the pain of letting go of what I've clung to. Or hung on to. Prejudice is a bulldog grip. It is clenched teeth. It is a spiteful bite that grips the past and its stale ideas as a protection against the present and its realities. It is hanging on to the imaginary security of fantasies that "me and my kind" are superior in some way. Healing follows a willingness to risk seeing, admitting, smiling at and saying good-bye to old generalizations. Then healing, forgiveness, love and reconciliation happen. The beliefs, attitudes, generalizations and stereotypes I carry with me into the next moment are my choice. Those prejudices and biases I keep with me are my responsibility. I am free—if I'm willing to accept the freedom inherent in humanness—to leave the past and its self-serving opinions behind me.

I have racist attitudes. I don't like discovering them in myself, so I've become expert at hiding and denying them. Now I know that freedom and healing come as I can own these attitudes, admit my inner confusion, confess my apathy, discard my myths and make a change. I have found that my prejudicial stuckness is connected to (1) my slowness to be moved by injustice done to others, (2) by my withdrawal from situations of human need into indifferent safety, (3) by enjoying my material resources without admitting that my gain often involves another's loss, (4) by profiting from government programs that privilege my kind and class while ignoring others. And that's only the beginning.

What function do prejudices perform for you? They serve some end or they would likely be dropped and forgotten. Become aware of what you're doing with your collection of racial labels and stereotypes. When you become aware—truly aware—of what you are doing and how you are doing it, you have a choice. You can choose to quit it. Or you can choose to excuse it and continue it.

Let your mind float freely for the next minute and fantasize with me.

It's morning. You're rubbing the sleep from your eyes after punching the alarm clock to silence, when you notice your hands. They're brown. Not their natural tan, but a deep dark brown. (Or if you're naturally black, imagine that the hands you hold in front of your eyes are suddenly white.)

You stumble out of bed and stand staring in dumb disbelief into the mirror. You're black. (White.) Overnight, through some unexplainable freak act of fate, you've become another, the other race.

The bacon-coffee smells of breakfast tell you that your wife (husband) is in the kitchen. What will she say or do as you enter? Will her eyes scream rejection? Will she recover with that phony smile (too wide, too long, too many teeth showing) that signals rejection while it speaks acceptance? The smile you've often given to people of other races?

The men in your car pool will be stopping by for you in 30 minutes. What will they say? And at the office, will there be a new distance separating you from your fellow workers? Will the job still be yours by tonight?

What of your friends? Will they be just as close as before? Your racist brother-in-law, how will you get along with him? And then there's your church; will you be welcome now? Or will the cold shoulder move you on to the side aisles and out of the door in a short time?

You look closely at yourself in the mirror. You've got to go out and face the world, but right now you're not happy about facing yourself, being the self you are becoming.

Fantasies such as this are one means of reversing our point of view—a way of getting unstuck where prejudging and prejudice have mired us fast.

To be able to see things from another's point of view is to be truly human, to be fully alive. To be willing to see life from others' perspectives is to begin to understand them and to know yourself. To be concerned about experiencing life from the vantage points—or disadvantage points—of other races and groups is to begin to awaken to life, to the world about you, to responsibility and to love.

Paul has some incisive words at this point. "Look to each other's interest and not merely to your own" (Phil. 2:4, *NEB*) and "If . . . life in Christ yields anything to stir the heart . . . any warmth of affection or compassion . . . [try] thinking and feeling alike, with the same love for one another, the same turn of mind, and a common care for unity" (vv. 1-3, *NEB*).

If we take his words to heart, they offer a call to radical empathy, to "try on another's skin, to listen until you have heard his or her point of view. Then get inside it. See how it fits for size. See how it feels to be there where he or she is. Then ask what love is inviting you to do."

Hubert Schwartzentruber, a pastor for decades in inner-city Saint Louis, speaks with a prophetic voice on linking Christian love and understanding to Christian action.

> The best gauge to determine what another's needs are is to take a look at what one's own needs are. I want to be free to make my decisions. If we then see someone else hindered from making free decisions, we must help to remove that which blocks decision-making and freedom for him.

> If I need a job, then my brother needs one too. . . .
>
> If I believe that my children need a good education, but many people through no fault of their own do not have my opportunities, then I have an obligation to help make quality education available for their children, too.
>
> If I have a need for a house for the safety of my family, then I must be concerned about the need of a man who, for a variety of reasons, does not have a safe place in which to house his family. . . .
>
> If it is for the welfare and the best interest of my family to have health care, then can I be a Christian without also doing something about the needs of those who have no way to obtain proper health care?[10]

Jesus was born in the most rigidly ethnic culture of all time; born in a fiercely nationalistic nation; born in Galilee, the most bigoted backwoods of that nation; born into a family of snobbish royal lineage; born in a time when revolutionary fanaticism fired every heart with hatred for the Roman oppressors; born in a country practicing the apartheid of rigid segregation between Jews and Samaritans; born in a world peopled with prejudiced, partisan, fanatical, intolerant, obstinate, opinionated, bigoted, dogmatic zealots—Roman, Samaritan and Jewish. Yet He showed not a trace of it.

Read and reread the documents of His life—the Gospels. There is absolutely nothing to indicate feelings of racial superiority, national prejudice or personal discrimination.

The wino looked up as he felt the hand on his shoulder. A dozen men had walked into his alley, stopped, circled around him.

"Sir," one said to the man who seemed to be in charge, "whose fault is it that this man is a wino? His own? Did his wife drive him to drink? Or was it his parents?"

"Forget the blaming games," the leader replied. "Ask instead, where can he go? What can he do now?"

Reaching out, he put his fingers under the man's stubbly chin. Their eyes met, caught, held.

"Come on," he said, "you're free to leave skid row. Here's a five. Go on over to the Y, shed your rags, shower, shave and go home."

Two hours later the man got off the bus in his old neighborhood.

"Hey, look. Isn't that Wino Willie?" an old neighbor asked.

"Can't be," another replied. "He's rotting in some alley by now."

"Sure looks like him."

"Yep," said Willie, "it's me!"

"What happened?"

"Dunno. This man says to me, 'Willie, you're free. Go on home. You're okay again!' I did. Here I am. I'm okay."

By this time a crowd had gathered. Family, old friends, two social workers, a probation officer, several local clergymen, a news reporter.

"What's going on?" they all asked. "What's with you?"

"Well, nine o'clock this morning, I'm just sleeping off my hangover from last night's half gallon of muscatel, and I'm feeling like the DTs are coming back, when this guy and his friends come up the alley. He talked to me like I was people. Told me I'm okay. Said I was free to put the old life behind me. I could go. I did. Here I am."

"You're putting us on," someone yelled.

"Yeah, it's a hoax. You weren't really a wino. What's your angle?"

"No angle," the guy replied. "I've been splotched for years. Now I'm sober."

"Impossible," a clergyman snapped. "Once an alcoholic, always an alcoholic."

"Could be," the man replied. "This I do know. Once I was wet, now I'm dry."

"Tell us again what happened," the crowd demanded.

"Why? Are you open to changing too? You want to taste a little of this freedom to be different?"

"Change? Nothing doing! You can't change human nature. You're no different. Just wait and see. You're Wino Willie and you always will be! Get out. Go back where you came from."

The downtown bus pulled in. Willie shrugged his shoulders, got on.

Back on the city street, one block from the bus depot, Willie ran into the man and his group of friends.

"They say I'm no different, that I can't change," Willie said. "I guess they're right. There really isn't any hope."

"What do you think?" the man asked.

"Me? I dunno. But I felt today like I really am different, like God touched me, like I really can be free. Like it's okay to be me."

"That's all true. You can go on being free. And God is with you, see?"

"Yes, I think I see. But my family, my friends, why don't they see it?"

"None are so blind as those who will not see!" (Compare John 9:1-41.)

FOR FURTHER EXPERIENCE

1. In the adventure of discovering, owning and finishing past experiences, affirm to yourself, to a significant other person, to God the following statements:

   (1) I do not deny the facts of my own past experiences. I do not need to overlook them; I will not distort and justify them. They are past expressions of my freedom to be me. They are no longer me. I am forgiven. I am free.

   (2) I, here and now, take responsibility for making my own decisions (I want information from others; I want understanding love from those near to me; I want to be aware of the way of Jesus); but I am fully responsible for my choices—satisfying or not—and I accept the consequences of my own behavior.

   (3) I recognize and respond to "God at work within me—giving me both the will to do and the power to perform." I own and choose "to work out this salvation with a proper sense of awe and responsibility" (paraphrase of Phillips' translation of Phil. 2:12-13).

2. Become aware of the prejudicial lines that you find running through your thoughts or appearing in your conversations. Track down the old habitual recordings, those taped messages from your past. You may not be able to erase these tapes, but you can pull the earplug, hit the off-switch, refuse to listen.

3. Become aware of the uses of humor to support old my-race-is-better-than-yours feelings. If you find yourself

telling any story that depends on racial comparison or competition, try owning what you're doing then and there. Try stopping in mid-story and declare your honest intentions to respect the differences that make others unique.

4. To break free to venture trust, love and understanding, consider these questions:

   (1) How am I stopping myself from seeing all persons—regardless of race, nationality, culture—as precious, just as I am precious?

   (2) How am I scaring myself from starting friendships, learning to appreciate the richness of differences, developing genuine empathy for others?

   (3) How am I stuck in viewpoints that are unfaithful to the Jesus I want to follow daily in life?

   (4) How am I blinding myself by selective exposure, selective attention, selective recall of data conflicting with my views?

   (5) How can I move into more open relationships that invite others to confront me where I am scared, stuck, closed, sometimes blind?

Peacemaking Is

Care-fronting,
Truthing,
Risking,
Growing,
Trusting,
Disagreeing,
Forgiving,
Challenging,
Accepting,
Demanding,
Canceling demands,
Owning responsibility,
Dropping blame,
Forgetting prejudice,
Acting in loving
Reconciling ways.
Making peace
is the Jesus way.

"For Christ is our living peace. He has made us both one [we and they] by breaking down the barrier and enmity which lay between us . . . he came and brought the good news of peace to you who were far from God and to us who were near."

St. Paul, Letter to Ephesians (2:13-15,17-18, *Phillips*)

9

PEACEMAKING:

Getting Together Again

There is a basic rule about peacemaking that is as predictable as gravity: *You can either make peace or get the credit for it. You cannot do both.*

Peacemakers learn that in order for peace to be restored between alienated people, both parties must own the process, take their own steps forward, consider the risks involved and accept the consequences for the agreed upon outcome. By the time they have done all this, the peace achieved belongs solely and fully to the participants, not to the peacemakers who assisted. In fact, the annoyances and leftover grievances often get laid at the mediator's door. If your need to be thanked is great, peacemaking is likely not a role you should seek. If your need is to be praised, then take sides and stir up party spirit. You will get the praise of those who follow. But peacemaking is bridge-building; and the purpose of a bridge is to be walked on; it exists for others to cross over and return.

The qualities that make peacemakers serve as sturdy bridges are not just their capacity to be caring, confronting, valuing people, although these are indispensable. The qualities of caring with as few conditions as possible and confronting with as great wisdom as is available come together in the peacemaker's suspending bridges between persons who have lost their vital connections.

Making peace is often a lengthy, tortuous, repetitious and tedious process requiring great patience and endurance. Peacemakers are persons who have developed a long-range vision and are able to see long-term goals. They are people of stubborn patience with a long view of human existence. When they speak of ordering their lives by principles, they are referring to those that have survived across time, that are universally applicable, that do not make exceptions for themselves and their kind of people. Universal principles are values that prize the equal worth of all humans, promote the equal human rights of all humankind and seek after justice for all of God's creation. These require the pursuit of long-term goals.

Immediate solutions have their place. They can reduce explosive tensions so that longer-range settlements can be negotiated.

Strategic solutions have their use. They can create a working agreement among parties that holds together until a more stable covenant can be made.

Temporary solutions are often the best we can achieve. In every state of concord lie the seeds of future conflict. In every state of conflict, the crucial elements for creating peace lie hidden. The normal rhythm of life is concord-conflict-concord-conflict-concord. Thus all solutions are temporary, all agreements tentative. Everything we achieve will be surpassed.

Peacemakers who have caught a vision of a lasting peace commit themselves not only to short-term gains but also to long-term goals. Peacemakers who take the long view recognize that the values that shape their decisions must be lasting values—values that transcend not only one's own culture, race and nation, but also one's own lifetime, century, millennium.

Nothing that is truly worth doing is ever completed in one generation's lifetime. Nothing that is truly worth attempting can be accomplished by one person, without the help, support, guidance and wisdom of the community. Nothing that will be lasting, that will endure, makes complete sense in any immediate situation, in any given moment in history.

So peacemakers prefer the long view and seek to set their consciences by those values that have depth in the history of humankind, that have breadth in their universal applicability, that have height in their accountability before God and all that is known through God's saving activity among His people.

Peacemakers have to be people of conscience; not the narrow conscience of self-accusing, self-negating perfectionism, but the broad, deep, high and long-visioned conscience of internalized values, convictions and commitments. This can make them appear a bit out of step with the status quo. They may in fact seem alienated, but that alienation occurs because they refuse to accept the alienation of an alienated community that has come to accept its own alienation as natural, inevitable and permanent.

"There are some rotten things going on at work: nepotism in promotions, an unequal pay scale, hiring and firing along racial lines. I'm never opening my mouth at work on how I feel about any of that," you tell your wife. "That bunch of blue-nosed conservatives would pick me clean like a flock of vultures."

"You're going to just stay mum, eh?" she asks.

"Yeah, buy me a turtleneck; I'm keeping my head in."

"But what does it do to your insides, to your soul, to keep your honest feelings hidden?" your wife asks.

"I don't know," you say. "It feels like an ulcer is growing on my conscience. My silence makes me look like a different man than I really am. I'd like to do better than that. But it would cost me everything to put what I really believe on the line."

"It would be the end of your being one of the guys."

"Or acting like one of the guys."

(Memo to self: "Better to remain silent and be thought a fool than to speak out and remove all doubt." Abraham Lincoln said that. He had to be joking. When it was time to speak, he spoke.)

Peacemakers have a uniquely centered commitment to conscientious behavior. Following the conscience is a uniquely human capacity, a truly human gift. It is a capacity that is often viewed with suspicion—"Who does she think she is?"—or mentioned in disdain—"She is striving for sainthood"—and rarely gains the immediate respect it deserves. Perhaps we have known too many people with strict and stinking consciences that restrict themselves and inflict their negative controls on others. However, the people you trust most and admire deeply are persons with an inner compass, a gyroscope in the soul that maintains their flight on a level trajectory, a personal global directional signal that keeps them on course. Conscience is not a faculty to be feared but a human quality to be prized and valued. In communities made up of conformists, someone with a conscience that varies from the mass mind may be viewed with suspicion or feared as a maverick or misfit, out of step with the rank and file and, since different, someone to be excluded.

"Conscientious wisdom" is the necessary quality. It is a conscience open to and committed to truth—a conscience informed by obedience to this knowledge. It is a willingness to examine and test all truth, to sift from the good the better, from the better the best, from the best the ultimate. Without *conscientious wisdom*, human beings endanger their humanity. Persons who have silenced their consciences live by the common, shared wisdom of their social group.

With a "conscientious *wisdom*," women and men become persons of integrity, sensitive to carefully examined values. A conscience unexamined, unexplored, untested can be a dangerous, even a deadly guide. No man will kill you with less compunction than a man who kills in obedience to his conscience. But a "conscientious wisdom" is a conscience open to, instructed by and committed to the highest truth man has found in all that is available to him. True, there are risks to following conscience. But more crimes have been committed in the name of duty and obedience to authority than in the name of conscience.

"Conscientious wisdom" is a kind of inner driven courage. It is the courage to be a responsible person, to believe in values, to see meaning in life; it is the courage to act with purpose and conform one's loyalties to one's true scale of priorities. This demands courage because following the conscience is a vulnerable act. It exposes a woman or a man to ridicule, anger, public rejection, shame, suffering, even violence.

(Consider Martin Luther King, Jr., a man who acted in conscience, a man who died for conscience sake. Days before his death I heard him say to a network newscaster, "If I choose to go on living by my conscience, I may survive at the most for five more years. I could compromise my conscience and perhaps live to be 80. Either way I die. The one way I would simply postpone my burial.")

(Consider Nelson Mandela, a man who emerged from Robben Island prison to be met by a welcoming crowd of thousands. Along with the whole watching world, I saw him raise a fist in the traditional sign of resistance and heard the angry roar of the crowd's response. Then he paused, silently listened to the voice of conscience. "At that moment, Jesus said to me," he has reported, " 'While you were in prison, you were free; now that you are free, why would you choose to be imprisoned by anger?' "

Then he spoke: "Friends, comrades and fellow South Africans. I greet you all in the name of peace, democracy and freedom for all! I stand here before you not as a prophet but as a humble servant of you, the people.")

(Consider Oscar Schindler. A Nazi war profiteer who came to Krakow, Poland, to manage a factory, Schindler realized that his Jewish employees were in danger of deportation to concentration camps to be exterminated along with the entire ghetto community. He began to aid them by bending the law, then by flouting it through shrewdly outguessing officialdom, bribing those with influence, falsifying documents, sacrificing all he owned, selling his wife's jewelry, giving aid at the risk of his own life, wife and family. By obeying conscience, he saved more Jews from the gas chambers at greater personal cost than any other single person during World War II, rescuing over 1,000 lives.)[11]

"Conscientious wisdom" is an act of faith, the faith that choosing the right thing is the best thing even though the cost seems staggering; the faith that time will vindicate the rightness of your act even though friends may condemn you now.

"That boy will be a CO only over my dead body," your husband says. His voice is rising.

"Don't shoot the messenger, I'm only reporting what our son's letter says."

"No son of mine is going to be a conscientious objector. If he doesn't want to volunteer, okay. But to declare himself a CO is senseless."

"It's his decision, not ours," you say.

"So you're supporting the kid's yellow or pink ideas," your husband snaps.

All kinds of words rush to your tongue in defense of your son. You bite them back; your son doesn't need your protection. Not against his own father. All he needs is an honest–and caring–mother, and you can be both without letting this divide your marriage.

"Dear, listen," you say. "I don't want this or anything else to come between us, understand?"

He nods.

"Let's stick to our own decisions and let our son make his. Neither of us agrees with all the choices he makes. We see this one from different sides, but that's okay."

"You want him to go yellow?" your husband asks.

"No, I want him to be a man who's free to choose his own values and live them. It's not only his right, but it's his responsibility to make decisions by his own conscience."

(Memo to self: Which is it? "Insanity is inherited—you get it from your children" or "True parents delight as their kids surpass them"?)

One of the most difficult moments of conflict in the conscience, when the demands of the surrounding world threaten to overwhelm conscientious choice, is the decision to participate or not participate in warfare.

If you were called to take part in a war that was in conflict with your personal conscience or had been declared unjust by trusted religious thinkers or was seriously questioned by other persons of careful thought—would you fight in it?

For example: If you had been a 20-year-old male citizen of Germany in 1940, would you have obeyed orders to machine-gun Jewish mothers, daughters and babies into a muddy trench grave? Or would you have fought in the Rhineland in unquestioning obedience if you knew that your regime was committing the mass murder of the Jewish race? Would you have the courage to refuse to fight in such an unjust war?

If you believe that more young Germans should have listened to their consciences and refused to obey orders (some did and died), then you hold them responsible for not questioning and objecting to the Nazi cause. When the genocide became clear, do you not believe that they had the human obligation to take a stand? Do you not find it incomprehensible that they made the choice to yield to the social political pressures to be executioners in terrifying tragedy?

How would you go about making the decision that war is or is not unjust? The 20-20 vision of historical hindsight would not be available. Nor would you likely have access to international opinion to challenge your own in a time of national crisis. When you come to such an actual decision, the responsibility rests on you and the community of friends you have come to trust; on your conscience, your best insight, your deepest convictions, principles and sense of truth. That places a great demand on the little voice within called conscientious wisdom.

How do people of good conscience go about discerning if a war is justifiable or not? How indeed do those who delegate the work of conscience to others (let better minds than mine think, weigh and decide) avoid this agonizing choice? Four classic options are apparent in most literature and biography. These are (1) blank check obedience; (2) holy war; (3) just war; and (4) nonviolent refusal of war.

The first option: A Blank-Check Decision. In giving my state a blank check, I am agreeing that any war that my government declares or enters into, I must support; and anything that my government asks, I'm responsible to obey. This option avoids all confrontation and silences the conscience in blanket or blind obedience.

We are responsible to obey our government, but are we not a part of that government's decision process? As citizens say yes in support, or no in disagreement, is not this the primary way in which they contribute to the integrity of the process? To obey responsibly is mature citizenship; to follow blindly is childlike membership. To give the state a blank check is essentially saying, "I'll go wherever, do whatever to whomever in obedience to any command." To abdicate conscience is to cease being a moral being—a truly human being. Is not the blind obedience of a blank-check decision intolerable to women and men of conscience?

A second option: The Holy War. Any war that defends our nation, which is established in justice and blessed of God, is holy, right and good. Our "cause is just, and conquer we must, because this is our motto, in God be our trust." There are evil empires that threaten us as a righteous nation, who despise our God-given freedoms, and we must resist them. The world can be clearly divided into the holy versus the unholy; and the ability to define clearly who is on the right side, on God's side, may obey with a clear and empowered conscience.

Is any nation's way of life totally holy—right? Has any nation in history deserved absolute unquestioning worship? Is nationalism worthy of becoming our religion? What is the point when patriotism becomes idolatry? The conscience cannot avoid such questions as it considers giving one's life to take the lives of others.

Sometimes this argument is stated, "Any war that defends our Christian nation, or Christendom against communism, or Christians against paganism, is automatically right." Muslims, Marxists, Maoists and Christians have gone to battle to advance their causes. But to justify a war as a "Christian crusade" is like talking of dry wetness or hot coldness. Where did Jesus Christ sanction war or approve violence? Where does He support participating in any way of hate, murder, violence and self-defense? Why did He lay down His life for the sake of others and refuse to take the sword even in self-defense? When did self-defense become a Christian virtue? How is it possible that the survival of our culture or of our own way of life becomes our sole remaining purpose? Who decided that this is a Christian virtue? What theology maintains that the ends justify the means? These are questions that trouble many persons' consciences as they hear the language of crusades, holy wars, righteous victories.

The third option: A Just War. Through the centuries, conscientious thinkers have agonized over the decision of how certain acts of violence or warfare may be justified. When a conflict qualifies by certain criteria as justifiable, it has been called "a just war." (*Just* is short for *justifiable.* No war can be truly considered "just" to all involved. In hindsight, many suspect that even the most "just war" was in the end, *just* war.)

This option necessitates confrontation with the facts leading up to the altercation, with the issues and interests at stake, with the means and methods of engaging in war. These are questions that finally must be explored by both the just and the unjust.

The Greeks originated the concept. "A just war" was any war declared by the Greeks against the non-Greeks, the Barbarians (a definition that combined blank check and holy war criteria). The Romans added the criteria that such a war must be (1) fought by soldiers not civilians, and (2) that it must be fought with just means for just causes. Christians (after Constantine baptized his entire army into the church in the year 300) adapted and extended these criteria for themselves.

Today, our standards for a just war have been set forth in our individual national constitutions, sharpened by the Geneva Conventions on warfare, and canonized in the creeds of most major Christian denominations. All agree on four major issues:

A just war must be (1) declared by a just authority, (2) fought for the one justifiable cause of establishing an orderly and just peace, (3) fought with justifiable proportionality between the amount of harm done and the benefits hoped for, and (4) fought by a just means, respecting noncombatants, and refusing inhumane weapons.

Do thoughtful Christians apply these principles when they are called up to fight? The record is not admirable. When wars are being waged by other nations, men and women of conscience are seldom hesitant to apply the criteria to judge the adversary. But when their own nation is involved, objectivity and motivation to think in clear moral terms tend to disappear as we excuse as necessary the bombing of random civilians as collateral damage, torture of prisoners to seek information, bypassing one's own laws by declaring martial exceptions or subcontracting abuses to allies that do not forbid them (special and extreme rendition it is called). Conscientious wisdom requires that Just War face its own self-chosen alternatives (1) either to endure the agony of deciding on the justice or injustice of war, or (2) to reject war. Just war thinkers and those who teach and practice nonviolence are on the same side. Both, in contrast to the two preceding positions, seek to limit war, reduce its use, end its injustices and save life, not excuse its becoming expendable.

History testifies to the difficulty of making this decision. I recall hearing Christian thinker John Howard Yoder comment in a public debate, "Did any Christians who held to a 'just war' doctrine ever conclude, after their government had committed itself to war, that the cause was unjustified and/or the means used were inappropriate and that therefore they should not serve? Such cases prior to Vietnam are few, or nonexistent. Once war is declared, the pressures to give blanket approval usually win out over any and all moral considerations. For pragmatic, expedient reasons, we choose 'to accommodate the integrity of love to the realities of life.' "

The fourth option: Nonviolent Refusal to Take Part in War. One can say no. When the conscience shudders at what is being demanded, the will can take a clear stand and say no to the demand that one take up arms to kill those who happen to live across the borders of other nations.

For the first 200 years of the Christian faith, Christ's followers, like their Master, renounced the sword, rejected war and died refusing violence even in self-defense. By the year 400, Augustine was approving a "just war"; by the year 1,000, "Christians" were fighting "holy" crusades; and by the twentieth century, churches and Christians were accepting violence as long as it served to stop the Nazis, the Fascists, the communists. During the two World Wars, bishops blessed bayonets and bazookas on both sides.

Christ Himself chose not to accommodate. He chose love as the final basis of action and acted consistently with that love. His associate, Peter, reports: "Indeed this is your calling. For Christ suffered for you and left you a personal example, so that you might follow in his footsteps. He was guilty of no sin nor of the slightest prevarication. Yet when he was insulted he offered no insult in return. When he suffered he made no threats of revenge. He simply committed his cause to the One who judges fairly" (1 Pet. 2:21-24, *Phillips*). "Yes, yes, well and good," many say in response to all this, "but I'm not Jesus. So He was absolutely sure of Himself, His principles, His position, His actions. But I can't be. So I accommodate and go to war. It stands to reason. It's just good sense! Christ's demands are too absolute, too narrow, too single-minded to work in an imperfect world."

Granted, all people and all human ways of life are imperfect. That's only another way of saying that we humans at our best are only relatively right. (That is not to say that right and wrong are relative.) It is the honest confession that no one of us has all the facts, all the insight, or possesses all truth. But that is no argument against Christ's way of nonviolence. It's the very reverse. If our best reasons and decisions are only partially or relatively good, then to take absolute and final actions—to snuff out lives with bombs, to napalm the earth bare of people, to exterminate one human or a whole city—all in pursuit of some imperfect relative good is irresponsible to Jesus Christ. If you choose to fight in wars you consider just, or if you, with me, choose to reject all war as outside the will of God, come to your decision in clear open exercise of your conscience, weighing all truth available to you. Anything less is being irresponsible to God, to humanity, to our nation, to our world, to our friends or to our enemies.

Obedience to conscience is the only true patriotism. Obedience to truth is the only true statesmanship.

"Happy are the peacemakers," Jesus once said, "because they are called God's children." They are God's children because they recognize the God of peace as their Father, the Prince of Peace as their leader and the way of peacemaking as the only Christ-like way of life.

Peacemakers risk stepping into moments of conflict to do curative peace work, to heal torn relationships and even do a bit of surgery by nonviolent action in protest, presence and service where needed. And they're also concerned about preventive actions of peacemaking. They look for building hostilities—and help to relieve them while they're still forming—before they reach the explosive stage. This preventive peacemaking requires that persons develop several special characteristics.

First, they look at people not in evaluation according to the worst thing they have done but by what they can become now. Like Jesus, these Jesus-people (peacemakers) look to see what new thing is possible for persons and communities and what form it could be taking. As the Bible puts it: "The very spring of our actions is the love of Christ. . . . This means that our knowledge of people can no longer be based on their outward lives (indeed, even though we knew Christ as a man we do not know him like that any longer). For if anyone is in Christ that person becomes a new person altogether—the past is finished and gone, everything has become fresh and new" (2 Cor. 5:14,16-18, *Phillips*, gender altered).

Second, peacemakers look for strengths in others and encourage them. They sense where there are constructive possibilities, gifts and talents lying dormant or ignored, and affirm them. As the Bible says: "For just as you have many members in one physical body and those members differ in their functions, so we, though many in number, compose one body in Christ and are all members to one another. . . .

"Let us have no imitation Christian love. Let us have a genuine hatred for evil and a real devotion to good. Let us have real warm affection for one another as between brothers, and a willingness to let the other man have the credit" (Rom. 12:4-6, 9-11, *Phillips*).

Look for opportunities of affirming, encouraging, helping release others to become all they can be in Christ. Love is the important thing, not brilliant insight into persons and personalities. Honesty is the indispensable thing, not attempting to avoid and gloss over the difficulty with a glaze of sweetness.

Loving with honesty, caring with confronting, truthing it in love—these are the keys. Concern for mutual fulfillment, joint opportunities for service and shared meaningful work is the real goal.

Peacemaking love works out the mathematics of justice.

Peacemaking love looks after each person's welfare and concerns. Peacemaking love sees each person as precious simply because he is. The word "love" falls short when we attempt to put all this freight within it. The biblical word for love, *agape* in the Greek, holds a rich constellation of meanings that sums up peacemaking love. Even it falls short unless we define it in reference to the person who fulfilled it most completely. The biblical model for love, Jesus, gathers all these meanings into one exemplary life. He is the model for the biblical teachings on loving relationships. Substitute the name "Jesus" for Paul's word "love" in his description of *agape* as caring concern and its meaning becomes more clear (see 1 Cor. 13).

Compare this portrait of embodied love with your understanding of *agape.*

Jesus was slow to lose patience,
was invariably kind,
was never jealous or possessive,
boastful or arrogant,
anxious to impress
or cherished inflated ideas
of His own rank, role or importance.
He did not act unbecomingly,
did not first seek His own interests,
did not pursue selfish advantage,
was not touchy and defensive;
did not keep account of wrongs suffered
nor gloat over the hardships of others.
His greatest joy was seeing truth come to life.

He accepted without retaliation,
all that people did or said to Him,
trusted without suspicion
all who approached Him,
believed without exception
the best for all who despaired.
He set no limits for what He could endure,
had no end point to His trust,
showed no fading of His hope.
His concern, respect and compassion
could outlast anything.

That gives the word "love" a personal face. Love is believable when it is embodied, incarnate, shown in the life of a person. The New Testament writers used this unusual word available to them to sum all this meaning they saw embodied and enacted in Jesus and poured it, in verbal shorthand, into the word *agape.*

Agape has been defined as "benevolent love," or "self-sacrificial love," or "disinterested love," or "self-giving love," or "unconditional-concerned-respect," or "neighbor-regarding love." The best definition that brings together the whole of biblical teaching on love is "equal regard." Valuing neighbor as self; prizing others as you prize yourself; seeing another as precious, worthful and irreducibly valuable is equal regard. These are action words, behavioral terms. Love is something you do. That's where our Western languages and Western ways of thinking shortchange us. For us, love is largely a matter of feelings, attitudes and emotional responses. *Agape* is action. It is equal regard acted upon in equal respect. It's a caring way of responding to people as persons of value. It's a confronting way of relating to people as individuals of infinite worth in God's sight and, therefore, in your own.

Love, as *agape,* is a warm, generous, self-forgetful commitment to act for the equal welfare of the other with no demand to be reciprocated, no need to be understood, no need to be praised, no need to be thanked and no need to enjoy the process.

Jesus valued the needs of the neighbor above all else. For Him, concern for others is the supreme value, the one thing of infinite worth. To be specific, to say that neighbor-love is infinitely superior in value to human knowledge is to say that no gain in human knowledge is worth even the smallest loss of neighbor-love. Or to say that neighbor-love is infinitely superior to any human achievements is to say that no amount of increase in human achievement and success is worth even the smallest decrease in Christ-like love.

The Jesus way of "love-in-actions-of-ultimate-concern-for-others" is the one course of action that is of infinite value. The Jesus way of loving-deeds is a lifestyle of living *for,* unshakably *for,* unconditionally *for,* unreservedly *for* the highest good *for* others. (Not in servile obedience to human whims but in concerned commitment to the highest good for others.)

Persons matter most. Those who live in the Jesus-way of love seek the highest good they can find (God's kingly rule) and share it in acted-out deeds of loving service, concern, respect and even self-sacrifice.

People matter most. Those who live in the Jesus-way of love act in mutual equal regard, not because it is the safe thing to do (it doesn't guarantee either success or survival), nor because it is the brilliant thing to do. (It seldom is the clever strategy or the pragmatic route of common sense.) They act in love because it is the Jesus thing to do, the Jesus way to live, the Jesus kind of loving. And since He alone has triumphed in the one permanent victory of all time—love acted out on a cross—His way is the only way that is certain to triumph totally, finally, ultimately, eternally.

So, for those who have come to accept this Jesus as Supreme Commander of creation and regard His words and His ways as the final authority on life and living, for such people this strange quality of love keeps cropping up. At unusual times, in unexpected ways, with unexplainable strength, this indefinable "something" appears.

It's the Jesus way of living, flawlessly demonstrated in the Jesus of the New Testament and made possible today by the Jesus strength-to-love that Christians call the Holy Spirit.

FOR FURTHER EXPERIENCE

1. Examine the four classic alternatives for the Christian conscience and participation in warfare. List benefits and liabilities of each. Affirm your own criteria for decision-making.

   (1) *The blank-check approach.* Whatever my government asks, I must do. The Bible commands obedience. I am not morally responsible for any acts done when under orders. (Nuremberg, Tokyo, the My Lai trials may disagree, but I obey.)

   (2) *The holy-war stance.* Any war that defends a Christian nation or Christendom against communism is a crusade for liberty, justice and righteousness. (Christians believed this in the Middle Ages. Some political and military leaders still claim it. It has had no continuing support by any Christian group except when swept along with nationalistic sentiment in times of great national stress.)

   (3) *The just-war conviction.* A war can be justified if (a) declared by just authority, (b) fought to bring a just and orderly peace, (c) fought with clear proportionality between amount of harm and benefits hoped for, (d) fought by just means, by combatants only, without inhumane weapons. (This is demanding—it demands the best use of conscientious wisdom, moral accountability and courage.)

   (4) *Nonviolent love.* War only creates the conditions for further wars. Violence breeds new and more vicious violent reprisals. Someone must break the cycle. Jesus called His followers to accept this challenge unconditionally. (Refusing to participate in violence is risky. There is no guarantee of either survival or success.)

Concluding Exercise

Choose a friend, partner or associate and test out the following assumptions as applied to your relationship. Work through the differences that arise.

Reflect on what you are learning about life together.

1. If conflict is natural, neutral and potentially creative, as well as possibly destructive, how can Christians best fulfill their roles as peacemakers?

   (1) By avoiding conflict?

   (2) By denouncing conflict?

   (3) By becoming creative persons who choose the love-fight and break through barriers by caring-confronting persistence?

2. If conflict can become a creative force for honest intimacy, how do we work at differences?

   (1) Discarding hidden strategies so that varied views and concealed disagreements can be exposed?

   (2) Increasing both trust and risk so that hidden factors can be shared and fearful people can experiment with openness?

   (3) Initiating love-truth, care-confront conversations where individuality can be expressed and then unity chosen and celebrated?

3. Since love is *the way* to perceive you as well as me, I want to love you enough to tell you the truth, and be truthful enough to demonstrate my love. I want to care-front; to truth it with you; to experience the love-fight.

Popular saying:

Religion is for those
Who are afraid of going to hell;
Spirituality is for those
Who have been there.

Unpopular sayings:

Spirituality is seeking inner peace;
Discipleship is peacemaking.

Spirituality celebrates the sunrise;
Discipleship sings in the dark.

Spirituality is discovering god in self;
Discipleship is seeing God in others.

Spirituality meditates by the sea;
Discipleship joins the dolphins.

10

SPIRITUALITY:

Seeing the Face of God in the Other

How we react to conflict expresses our spirituality of the road.

How we respond when, as we say, we hit a rough stretch, or as the English say, a hard patch, reveals our core values about the spiritual journey

If ours is a spirituality of self-fulfillment, self-discovery, self-actualization, the conflict will focus primarily on the self, on its personal threat to safety and security or on the concern for avoiding shame or public defeat.

If ours is a spirituality of obedience to divine command and the pursuit of God, the conflict ultimately turns on what is right, absolute, eternal and how it will be defined, applied, demanded.

If ours is a spirituality of love for neighbor as the practice of love for God, then there will be a deep concern for justice, mutuality and the common good.

These three options map the three major streams of spiritual quest; they reveal profound differences in the goal of that quest. These are not incidental differences; they shape the primary motivations in dealing with tensions in relationships and contrasts in perspective—they shape how we face and find our way through conflict. They go to the heart of spiritual experience and its expression in the issues of daily life.

The stream of spirituality down which we flow is of crucial, pivotal importance in how we approach the conflicts that inevitably come into our lives. This will become more clear as we look at the wide spectrum of spiritualities by using this simple but profound threefold vision of the goals of the search for inwardness and its impact on our relationships.

The three great streams of spirituality are those that focus primarily on: (1) knowing the self (spiritualities that are concerned with fulfilling the self can be called *mono-polar*); (2) knowing God (spiritualities that are concerned with the soul finding and relating to God add a second pole, so are *bi-polar*); or (3) finding self by knowing God and neighbor (*tri-polar* spiritualities see the indivisibility of concern for God, self and others and invest deeply in all three). They recognize that those who seek the face of God find it in the faces of friend, neighbor and, sometimes, stranger and enemy.[12]

These produce three very different forms of spiritual practice.

1. *Mono-polar spirituality* awakens self-discovery in the seeker, initiates self-development and encourages the exploration of depth. Its call, like that of the ancient Greeks, is "Know thyself," and the search for a higher, better self leads the person to seek the inviting possibilities of finding shadows of the transcendent in oneself, in one's appreciation of beauty, nature, music, art, poetry, reverence for the earth, the environment and all that surrounds and enhances one's life. The focus is still on the enrichment and enlightenment of the self that comes through spiritual breakthrough.

2. *Bi-polar spirituality* begins as one encounters the Transcendent Other, God, and seeks to know God as the path to true self-knowledge. It finds that one knows the self through knowing God; sees the self in a radically new light by looking at experience from the

eyes of God ("viewing one's life from the balcony" it is sometimes called). This is the soul of traditional spirituality in much of historical Christianity as well as in many parts of Judaism before Christianity and in much of Islam after it, although in each of these traditions there are streams of practice that venture on to tri-polar spiritual life. Bi-polar spirituality is the most frequently taught and practiced form in the mainstream of Christianity. Jesus did not teach it. His major problems and conflicts occurred with those that did.

3. *Tri-polar spirituality* sees that the love of God cannot be split from love of the neighbor; it discovers that only in love of God and other do I come to actually know my true self in right relationships of reverence for both God and humanity. It takes the biblical question seriously, "If I do not love my brother or sister whom I have seen, how can I love God whom I have not seen?" (1 John 4:20).

Let's pause to seek a better understanding of all three.

Style 1: Mono-polar Spirituality of Self-fulfillment

Mono-polar spirituality is present in popular music, television programs, new age retreats, workshops and most popular literature about spirituality as self-fulfillment and self-discovery. A recent study in the San Francisco Bay area of California identified almost 200 discrete types. The wide interest in new forms of spirituality, often without religious attachment or interest, reveals the keen interest in finding meaning to life, direction for living and strength beyond the resources of one's private self. We can and indeed should be delighted when anyone begins to explore spirituality, and not disparage or discourage movement toward the transcendent in any of its many forms. We do well to remember that it was said of Jesus that He was so gentle and caring for life that He would not snuff out "a smoking wick" or "break a bruised and brittle reed" (see Matt. 12:20). Mono-polar spirituality takes the first steps of opening the soul in the beginning of soul-making. It seeks a spirituality that discovers the sacred within, the holy in nature, the numinous mysteries of one's inner depths and their connection to the universe. It is, to quote bestsellers that introduce a new age of spirituality, "getting back in touch with your soul," "journeying to the best and highest place within," "living in your sweet spot," "reverence for life, for self, for nature, for your higher possibilities."

"I belong to a church of one, and my cathedral is that made of the trunks of the redwoods where I go walking to calm my soul," the young woman explains. "I have found a spirituality of my own—mossy banks, towering trees, crunching needles and leaves. When I lose myself in a virgin forest, something eternal speaks to me from a millennial tree, from rocks that formed in primeval periods. I feel my own eternal nature as one with all that surrounds me."

"I am a very spiritual person. I have a deep sensitivity to the meaning of life that stretches far back into the past. I have discovered that in previous lives, I was once a Norse shaman, then a holy man along the Ganges, a priestess in a Greek monastery, a healer who headed a community of Celtic nuns. I am learning to tap into this power, find the goddess within, and call out the spiritual healing of illnesses that people do not yet know that they have."

Style 2: A Bi-polar Spirituality of Knowing God

Bi-polar spirituality begins in meeting God; it is the encounter with One who is present in our lives and calling us toward relationship. For some it is primarily a matter of right thinking, an intellectual reorientation of life with the assurance of God's providence and sovereign control; for others it is predominately emotional and experiential as they claim God as co-traveler and daily presence in their personal world. Bi-polar spirituality lies on the other side of a life-death experience. God dies—the god of our own creation and celebration—and a part of our self dies with it. We encounter a sovereign God, a God who is truly other, who stands above all human manipulation, beyond our strategies of control. It is frightening to experience the death of one's private, individualized magical Protector-Provider who rescues me and mine as special cases, and even more frightening to meet the God who is beyond all the stand-ins we create.

"For me it was a personal breakthrough. I had not grown up believing in God or being involved in religious practices. Then something inexplicable happened to me—I discovered that all my arguments for a natural universe without a supreme being made sense no longer. In my practice of medicine, I saw people face illness and death with courage and trust. I started exploring the writings of thinkers who were believers, and one night I found myself praying. I have no explanation for what happened except that God met me at 2:00 A.M., spoke to me in a way that connected things in me that had never been linked before. Since then, I am a believer."

"I have always known about God, from my earliest memories. I have always wanted to know God, as far as I can recall. I had parents who loved God. Somewhere along the way, I came to know and love Him too. God is the center of my life—of my spiritual life of prayer, trust in His guidance, confidence that He cares for me and those I love."

Style 3: A Tri-polar Spirituality of Love for God and Neighbor

Tri-polar spirituality dawns with the realization of the inseparable unity of love for God and love of neighbor. It unfolds in the recognition of the presence of God in the other. Love for God and neighbor, two aspects of one and the same love, are inextricably united. As Jesus taught, the greatest commandment is to love God, the second is its likeness, to love the other, who is the image of God to us. It continues in the radical, subversive walk of living out love without conditions, exceptions, exemptions; it ends in following the ultimate dissident exemplar, Jesus, who said, "A new commandment I give to you, that you love one another as I have loved you." Some love is rational, but Jesus asks for a love that is post-rational; some commitments are reasonable and logical, but Jesus requires a commitment that is post-logical. There is an inevitable death experience at the entry boundary to tri-polar faith and practice. Self as supreme good puts up a significant fight for survival; surrendering the future into another's care and protection, even if that other is God, is not simple. The commitment to place one's life in God's hands does not come easily.

"I think I first saw the face of God in a teacher who cared about me and my future. I came from a fractured family where everyone had to look after himself, look out for herself. So when someone valued me—it was only a few words, but they were the right words at the right time—it was like God had spoken to me. I started going to the church where I heard that teacher attended. I found other people who saw something in me, believed that my life mattered. I can name three who were the face of Jesus to me. That is how I came to faith, and it is how I want to live my faith, caring about others; showing how important they are to me, giving God a face to them that they can believe."

"I was reading the Gospels when the words of Jesus blew away my old understandings of spirituality. He had this radical understanding of giving a love that does not draw lines between those who deserve and those who do not, on living a life of love that treated the neighbor—the poorest of neighbors—with the same honor and respect that one gave to God. I realized that the way I loved my neighbor, the stranger, the enemy, was the actual equivalent to the way I loved God. It was a whole new concept of living with concern for the welfare of all about me, that this was the Jesus way. I was totally captivated. I have never escaped."

Tri-polar spirituality, as Jesus taught and lived it, places love for the neighbor and concern for the self on the same level. It produces a life turned outward toward others. Through this love for others, given in His way, we love God. Of the three types of spirituality we have identified, the first has the longest history—religion as a way of controlling and domesticating a frightening and puzzling world; the second is the path of the standard religious life that works out a relationship of personal, often individual care, support, guidance that we call "salvation." The third is the radical way of the disciple, the way of taking love, service, sharing, reconciling, peacemaking with total seriousness.

We might visualize these three types of spirituality as three interlinked circles, as three points on a triangle; but it is useful to see them on a continuum that also allows for exploring the spaces between that also have styles of spirituality and characteristics that are highly familiar. The midpoint between mono-polar and bi-polar is a spirituality of creating a god in one's own image; it is called "mirror of self spirituality." And between bi-polar and tri-polar there is a spirituality of concern for others, benevolent spirituality. These differing paths will become more clear in the diagram on the following page.

A further description of the two middle-ground spiritualities that fall at 1.5 and 2.5 will clarify the ways we combine the poles to build our own compromise alternatives—in 1.5, to have a god but to make this a god who fits us, meets our needs, exists for us; in 2.5, to seek to do God's will in as far as it is humanly possible without demanding what seems impossible. These two reveal how we may struggle between the wish to stay in the familiar spiritual place (our comfort zone) or risk moving to a more demanding spiritual path (outside our zone of comfort).

Mono-polar, Bi-polar, Tri-polar Spirituality

1	1.5	2	2.5	3
Mono-polar Spirituality	**Mirror of Self "My own god."**	**Bi-polar Spirituality**	**Benevolent self that serves God**	**Tri-polar Spirituality**
Know thyself	My god and I	God alone is God	Serve Sovereign God	Love of God and other
Spirituality of in-search and self-discovery.	Spirituality of wish fulfillment and projection.	Spirituality of God-encounter. God as Other.	Spirituality of gratitude, service, and neighbor love.	Spirituality of radical *agape* and enemy love.
I am a church of one, of me	God is on my side, our side	I know true self as I know God	As I love God, I care for others	I love God only as I love enemy
Self as primary locus of the holy	Create your God who fulfills and aids	Death and rebirth: god becomes God	Worship the provident God	Follow the God of Jesus Christ
Prayer: centering for meditation and self-discovery.	Prayer: claiming personal success and prosperity.	Prayer: surrender to the Other and the Divine commands.	Prayer: Intercession for others that cares and serves.	Prayer: humble yieldedness to the way of Jesus.
In conflict, take your own side seriously. Your life matters; prize and defend it.	In conflict, trust that God is on your side working out your best interest.	In conflict, be sure you are on God's side; the two of you are ultimately right.	In conflict, be kind to the other side; be gracious and give wise, generous care.	In conflict, equal concern for both sides, mutual care for self and neighbor
Win in conflict!	Manage conflict!	Control conflict!	Resolve conflict!	Transform conflict!
Forgiveness is the gift that you give to yourself.	Forgive to get free, to evict the other, to not be held hostage.	Forgive if you wish to be forgiven; if you will not, God cannot.	Forgive as an act of generosity, kindness and compassion	Forgive to regain a sister or brother in right relationship.
Focus is on Me, My	Focus is on We/They, our kind	Focus is on Thou	Concern for Them	God-you-me; a new we

Mirror of self-spirituality (1.5) sees a face in the spiritual looking glass, feels a presence beyond self, recognizes that God is in all, behind all, acting for us in all. This spirituality of a familiar, friendly, kindly Deity finds comfort in its similarity to father, mother, heroes, nation and even the self. We look into the mirror and see our own national, racial, ideal image and come to trust it as divine. This God of wish fulfillment is a normal part of childhood, and as it continues into adulthood, this God of our creation and likeness extends the qualities of Santa or Superhero, and tends to reflect our own race, culture and belief system. It supports us in our limitations as a good magical friend. This is an inevitable development as the soul reaches upward for the transcendent and finds in this higher level we call "the Beyond" the hope of one who guarantees our safety and security, offers comfort and companionship in fulfillment of one's deepest desires and highest goals. Later we come to ask what the Deity, God, may truly want of us, not how we can get what we want from the divine provider and rescuer when we are in trouble. "My God is my own," people often say in defense of their flight from a religious community and its inevitable accountability demands. Or they protest, "I have my own God," in response to another's challenge or in protest to another's affirmation of faith.

Mirror of self-spirituality speaks familiarly, possessively, of "my God" and looks to this God to bless self, family, nation. "God Bless ____(my nation)" can be prayed in fear or in confident certainty that God is, obviously, on our side. "God Bless America," "Rule Britannia," "*Gott mit uns*" are creedal confessions of faith that affirm the security provided to us by a tribal or national deity. The 1.5 spirituality provides us with a generic god, the national tribal-god invoked at political conventions, enlisted as support in elections, named as final clinching point in presidential speeches, stamped on our coins, dropped into pledges, constitutions and declarations—a god who is on our side, not a God who confronts us with our misuses of His name, misappropriation of His intentions, mistaken ideas about His will and way.

The death that occurs at the boundary where we enter the second pole and meet God who is Other results in the shattering of the "mirror of self" image that blesses the self ("I'm okay") and smiles graciously as one "forgives oneself." The encounter with a God who stands beyond our "mirroring god" challenges our unquestioned certainties of eternal safety and security guaranteed by the deal struck with "our own god" to save us on our terms. This step initiates the slow death of childish "wish fulfillment" faith that projected its sacred ideal self on the heavens. The death of spiritual narcissism, of a vain nationalism of "God's chosen people," of a private ownership of the God who guarantees my inviolate existence may happen with the collapse of spiritual self-strategies when one encounters a God who is Other. For many, this is so frightening that they can conceive of a God who is somewhat other, but still with a "god-image" that bears a remarkable familiarity with my kind of people, an undeniable similarity to the self.

When God dies, *God* appears. Leo Tolstoy wrote of this experience of the death of God:

> If the thought comes to you that everything that you have thought about God is mistaken and that there is no God, do not be dismayed. It happens to many people. But do not think that the source of your unbelief is that there is no God. If you no longer believe in God in whom you believed before, this comes from the fact that there is something wrong with your belief, and you must strive to grasp better that which you call God. When a savage ceases to believe in his wooden God, this does not mean that there is no God, but only that the true God is not made of wood.[13]

When hope is lost, true hope appears. The hopes of our immature years—the confident optimism, the naïve positivism, the superficial assurance of youth—are laid aside. The future is not a golden path to the sapphire stairs leading to the lavender clouds of serene safety and success. Life is not the guaranteed perfection of our dreams. This world is not the best of all possible worlds. We have known this yet we do not *know* it as long as we follow the will o' the wisp of our emotional gods who lure us onward with the promise of fulfilling our desires.

Benevolent spirituality (2.5) springs from gratitude; it comes in consequence of the bi-polar spirituality that leads us to share the grace we have received so that benevolence and kindness result. Having encountered God the Other who loves all others, it reaches outward in pity and compassion for others. It is motivated by gratitude for grace received and seeks the wellbeing of others in thankful response to the generosity of God. It sees love for others as the *agape* of benevolence; it seeks to fulfill the divine intentions for humanity in as far as humanly possible and in accord with the limits of human frailty. It has its limits defined by common sense, the right to survival, and self-defense and rational self-protection. When personal survival is threatened, then love of enemy is redefined into a different kind of "love" that permits our bombing the enemies' homes, schools, family, children. The spiritual soldier can now do this with an absence of hate, however, carrying out the violence as a sad but acceptable alternative necessary for the nation's way of life, its economic stability, energy needs, multinational corporations all explained as "our freedoms." Tri-polar spirituality recognizes that since my life is in God's loving hands, I can never take my enemy's life into my hands; since my enemy stands in need of God's grace, as I also stand, I cannot take his life without taking away his opportunity to encounter that grace; since whatever I do to the least of Christ's fellow human beings, I do to Him. It realizes that Jesus' call to enemy-love is a call for us to be like our Father in heaven who loved us and reconciled us to Himself while we were His enemies (see Rom. 5:10). It asks, "When I kill my enemy, do I destroy my way to God—do I, in fact, kill God?" Hard question. It is not easy to follow Jesus to tri-polar spirituality.

"Why do you work at reconciliation when it is so demanding?"

"I do it because it is the most important task in the world."

"Really? Bringing people together, and helping them make peace, is more important than your survival?"

"Rather, it is the only way any or all of us will survive."

"Hmmm . . ."

When a spirituality of self-fulfillment is the primary base of operations in your world of relationships, it gives you a reason for taking care of yourself, of not allowing abuse, of refusing to do things that are harmful to your self and your part in any conflict. This is basic, necessary, appropriate self-care. This pole must be present in all three streams of spirituality. We must know ourselves; we must attend to our needs, drives, hopes, dreams, motives and direction in life. This pole is indispensable. It creates a strong position of self-care, assertive strength and willing action for what is good. (Every position casts a shadow; some shadows are longer than others. This position throws the shadow of self-interest to darken any interest in the other's needs or wants. The shadow of self-absorption can lead to either flight from real contact with others or self-protective moves that vary from yielding to be safe to fighting to be the top competitor or winner.)

When a spirituality of Divine command is the basis for your responses to conflict, then you will seek to do what is fair, just and right. You will look for what is the best outcome, the highest goal, the clearest vision of good will, the welfare of all people, the health of community. (It also has its shadow side: it tends to make one "right" and the other "wrong" in either/or thinking; it often has an agenda it presses on others without listening and with little negotiation possible. It seeks "my way" as the right way, sometimes insists that "My way is Yahweh." It needs the benevolence that comes as the result of humble gratitude.)

When a spirituality of equal love for self and other is the ground for working through conflict, you will seek to understand issues that arise between you with concern for the welfare of both sides; you will seek to satisfy the interests of both sides with a commitment to find a third way—not my way, not your way, but our way. You will find that through caring about the relationship and taking care of the process of working at the conflict, you are caring for the other person and his or her needs. (This too has a shadow side. It is demanding, so it may exhaust you at times. It is costly, so it may mean giving up some of your wants to find a greater good. It is dangerous at times, since you may put yourself in the middle where the blows are falling hard and fast, and you get most of them in trying to make peace.)

The spirituality that grounds us, empowers us, opens us to envision healing of relationships is the most crucial factor in our being effective peacemakers—becoming what Jesus called the "children of God" (see Matt. 5:9,45), Jesus offers an alternative way through conflicts, a way of forgiving and reconciling. As was noted in the chart of the three spirituality polarities, the three main paths that direct most forms of spirituality offer very different views of forgiving.

Self-oriented spirituality sees forgiveness as "the gift you give yourself," and its goal is to set yourself free from all resentment and heal yourself.

God-oriented spiritualities see forgiveness as a requirement for being forgiven, an obligation for us all if we hope to be accepted and released from our obligations that we cannot pay. It takes forgiveness as a duty, an act of obedience, a necessary step toward being "right with God," whether or not it results in your being right with the brother who offended you or the sister who hurt you. It holds up pardon as the primary model. It views forgiving as letting go, setting the other free in order to be free oneself.

Love of neighbor and Love of God spirituality works for reconciliation. It sees forgiving as the last step of healing, as recognizing that change, repentance and reaching out again is genuine, and right relationships have been restored or achieved. It is not focused on self and making sure that self is 'okay,' or on personal perfection and "Am I 'okay' with God, and is God 'okay' with me?" It is focused on our finding one another again, of being "okay" with each other, knowing that as we are reconciled we are discovering that God is present with and between us; when we are not reconciled, we have shut Him out.

A spirituality that seeks a balanced practice of love of self, love of God and love of neighbor may seem terribly demanding; in reality it is incredibly rewarding. It may seem like a very costly pathway that requires giving up a part of the self. So it is, but the part of the self that is given up is a part we need to part with. It may seem like a fool's venture, but no one is a fool who risks what cannot be kept to gain what cannot be lost; never question an act of courage that gives up what is temporary to gain what is lasting.

One of the scribes approached him, . . . and he put this question to him:

"What are we to consider the greatest commandment of all?"

"The first and most important one is this," Jesus replied— " 'Hear O Israel: The Lord our God, the Lord is one: and thou shalt love the Lord thy God with all thy heart, and with all thy soul, and with all thy mind, and with all thy strength.' The second is this, 'Thou shalt love thy neighbour as thyself.' No other commandment is greater than these" (Mark 12:28-31, *Phillips*).

APPENDIX 1

CONFLICT BEHAVIOR SURVEY

The Conflict Behavior Survey is a testing instrument that will provide useful readings of your preferences for (1) a particular way of responding; (2) the pattern of preferences as you move from one style to another; and (3) the comparison of which conflict behaviors are most developed and employed versus those that are less practiced and seldom used. Follow the instructions on how to take it several times while thinking of different relationships so that you can contrast and compare how you respond in differing situations.

When a conflict occurs, which response is more effective—to differ clearly, to deny safely, to defer quickly, to defend vigorously or to defeat triumphantly? We all have a repertoire of conflict behaviors learned from early models, difficult struggles and tough experiences. This test will help you identify your preferences for particular styles.

To get the maximum benefit from this test, you will be taking it twice, choosing two different situations or relationships. Focus attention on a situation where your strong preferences differ from those of another person—spouse, friend, coworker, opponent. Choose two such relationships and take the test twice, answering according to how you most often respond to that particular person or situation.

The paired statements that follow offer possible behavioral options for each set. Circle option "A" or "B" to choose the response that is more close to your usual behavior. If neither fits, please select the one you might be more likely to choose or use if these were the only options possible in that situation or relationship.

As I think of how I handle differences:

with ______________________________ *(take test thinking of situation or person A)*

with ______________________________ *(retake test thinking of situation or person B)*

with ______________________________ *(retake test thinking of situation or person C)*

1. **A** When we differ, I usually look for a solution where we can each come halfway.
   B When we differ, I try to hear all of the other's concerns and then share my own.

2. **A** I have a strong commitment to press for my values and goals.
   B I look out for the other's feelings so that conflict will not threaten our relationship.

3. **A** When we differ, I see if I can go along with the other's goals and point of view.
   B It is often better to remain silent in conflict situations than to speak out.

4. **A** I try to work through differences as carefully as possible, respecting both our needs.
   B I try to find a balanced and fair share of gains and losses so that both sides gain something.

5. **A** I always ask the other to help in designing a solution to our problem.
   B I save myself a lot of stress by just avoiding unnecessary tensions.

6. **A** If the issue is very important to the other, I back off and let her/him win.

   B In conflict, if I take a lot of time to think over issues, they often resolve themselves.

7. **A** I am not afraid to take a firm stand in spelling out and sticking with my goals.

   B As soon as possible, I try to get both of us to put our interests and issues on the table.

8. **A** If I avoid controversial positions, I do not get into trouble with others.

   B If it makes the other happy, I can go along with most things that come up.

9. **A** If I come halfway, it will help the other to be more willing to come to meet me.

   B When I feel that I understand what is clearly right, nothing can make me compromise.

10. **A** I like to win arguments, so I put myself fully into a debate.

    B Life is too short to go around creating unpleasant tensions over personal issues.

11. **A** I am willing to give up some of my goals in a trade-off with the goals of the other.

    B I think most differences are not worth worrying about or struggling over.

12. **A** I find it's better to sacrifice my own wishes and go along with those of the other.

    B I look for a compromise where we each come halfway and both win something.

13. **A** I want us both to be satisfied, so I check again to understand your point of view.
    B I do not hesitate to press for my way when I believe it is the right or the best way.

14. **A** I can be firm in getting my way when it is clearly the right way.
    B I look for a solution that allows us both to at least win something if not everything.

15. **A** I look at the other's way, reconsider my way, then look for a creative third way.
    B My greatest concern is that nothing will impair or destroy our relationship.

16. **A** I dislike controversy. I find I can avoid it by taking tentative, not hard positions.
    B I think it's wise to find a healthy way to share in a compromise.

17. **A** I'll let the other win some important goals if I can reach some of mine.
    B Frankly, a lot of differences don't really matter, they are not worth worrying about.

18. **A** I will not risk our relationship just to assert or demand my point of view.
    B I press to make my points first–I think it's good to take a clear position.

19. **A** On issues that seem to matter more to the other than to me, I go along with the other.
    B It's often a matter of a trade-off; if I give a little, often the other will give a lot.

20. **A** If I am not firm in holding to my goals, others take advantage of me.
B I want the other to help in working out the solution so we both own it.

21. **A** If it's a choice between endangering the relationship or giving in, I prefer to give in.
B I don't like tension, so I do what is necessary to avoid situations that arouse my anxiety.

22. **A** I do all I can to avoid hurting the other person's feelings.
B When I have taken a clear and responsible position, I do not back down easily.

23. **A** Above all, I try not to hurt the other person's feelings or self-esteem.
B I listen to the other's perspective and I risk sharing mine so that we can work it out.

24. **A** I stand by my goals in an argument or conflict when winning is necessary.
B I think I should give a little if I expect the other to give a bit in return.

25. **A** I ask for the other person's ideas and I make sure my own are heard.
B I point out the weaknesses of the other's position and the strengths of mine.

26. **A** I think it is important for both of us to get our issues clearly expressed and understood.
B In conflict, if it's possible to put off dealing with it until later, it is wise to take time.

27. **A** I'm happy if others take the lead in resolving difficulties or differences.
    B I avoid talking about our disagreements and focus on the areas where we agree.

28. **A** When I negotiate differences, I start by considering the other's wishes, then share mine.
    B I like to focus on both sides of any problem to get a double view of issues and interests.

29. **A** I always try to start from the middle—civilization is built on wise compromise.
    B There's nothing wrong with asserting my wishes—if I don't, who will?

30. **A** I do not lose hope that we can find a mutually satisfactory solution.
    B I often back off and let the other take the lead in resolving the problem.

Scoring instructions: Take the test two or three times as recommended, using different colors or different marks—check, circle, x. Add the choices in each column to find the total for the two or three situations or relationships you chose to envision. Then chart the items on the box graph, using a dotted line, straight line, dashes in line or use colored ink pens to differentiate the pattern of scores from the various selected situations.)

1.	B	A			
2.			B	A	
3.			A		B
4.	A	B			
5.	A				B
6.			A		B
7.	B			A	
8.			B		A
9.		A		B	
10.				A	B
11.		A			B
12.		B	A		
13.	A			B	
14.		B		A	
15.	A		B		
16.		B			A
17.		A			B
18.			A	B	
19.		B	A		
20.	B			A	
21.			A		B
22.			A	B	
23.	B		A		
24.		B		A	
25.	A			B	
26.	A				B
27.			B		A
28.	A	B			
29.		A		B	
30.	A				B

Answer key: Mark each of your answers in the long boxes given using different colors or marks to designate the different relationships you have chosen to examine in the survey.

Total scores

1. (e.g., boss) ______ ______ ______ ______ ______
2. (e.g., spouse) ______ ______ ______ ______ ______
3. (e.g., friend) ______ ______ ______ ______ ______

Conflict Scoring Graph. Mark scores and connect with lines for profile

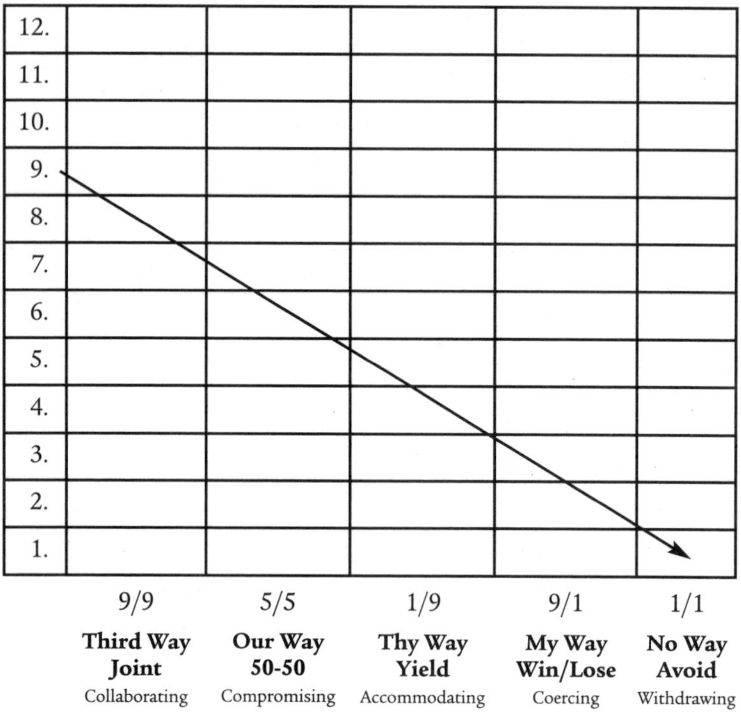

Interpreting Your Scores

The order of preferences you chose will be indicated on the Conflict Scoring Graph. The highest score indicates your first response to conflict with the person or in the situation you have named. The second highest is the next backup position that you move to when the first is unsatisfactory or not successful, and so on throughout all five.

The number of points between options indicates how long you continue to use a particular style before you move on to the next. A very high score on one style, for example, indicates a very strong reliance on that particular behavior.

The diagonal line indicates the preferred sequence. It is considered preferable, but not as an ideal or a necessary condition for all cultures or contexts, to proceed from 9/9 to 5/5 as a negotiating point, attempting to move back up to 7/7, 8/8 and 9/9. If this is not effective, then the third option should be 1/9 to build the relationship. If it is lost, all is lost. Only when the other refuses to affirm the ongoing relationship does one move to 9/1 to clarify where one's position on the issue truly stands. Leave 1/1 to the last to be used when all else fails, if at all.

In different situations the order may be very different. In rescuing a child from an abusive situation, the order may be reversed. In picking a restaurant with a spouse or sibling when you have no real preference, 1/9 is fitting; in picking an item to split on the menu, 5/5; in letting the other pick up the check when it is their turn, 1/9; in refusing to eat the entrée that is spoiled food, 9/1 is the right way to go.

When there is a flat line with all scores equal or nearly equal, the profile is called "a situational 5/5." This means that the person has an equal openness to all styles, equal skills in each and chooses the response appropriate to the situation. This makes the person very flexible and highly adaptive. However, those near are unable to predict how the person will relate; those in conflict with them are unsure who will answer the door—the compromiser, the competitor, the yielder, the collaborator or if no one will come to meet them. It is preferable to have at least two styles that are stronger than the others so that others have some confidence in your characteristic way of dealing with differences.

A high score on 1/1 that avoids, withdraws, evades, postpones as long as possible takes precedence over all else since it ends the interaction and leads to inaction. A high score on 9/1, coercing, forcing, compelling, often indicates a higher need to control or manage others. This is not necessarily strength, because it may hide a fear of being vulnerable or negotiable as weakness. The 9/1 may fear challenge, see compromise as sin and evil, insist on either/or solutions that are oversimplified as good over bad, right or wrong. A high score on 1/9, as accommodating, yielding and relinquishing, is thought to put relationships first, but it often builds a relationship of being coopted or controlled and does not possess the healthy balance of give and take, mutuality and reciprocity.

Change and growth are a matter of finding models, thinking more collaboratively, learning new responses, testing them with trusted people, getting the feedback that encourages their regular use, and discovering new outcomes. Sometimes it is a matter of combining behaviors that are already familiar (for those who have high scores on both accommodating and coercing, and swing back and forth, they can learn to do both simultaneously in caring support and confronting exploration of goals). The old way of expressing support, BUT the goal is replaced with support AND the goal that links the two sides in balanced ways of standing with the other while standing for a point of view.

APPENDIX II

THE ART OF RECEIVING CRITICISM

Hearing and heeding criticism usefully and authentically is a central evidence of maturity. Receiving confrontation without becoming reactive is an art that we learn slowly, but it is the other side of the communication process when differences get addressed. To hear criticism clearly and nondefensively, the following skills can be learned and internalized.

(1) *Listen to the criticism with suspended judgment,* not with the instant insight of self-judgment or self-defense. It is common to speed up thoughts and feelings when being criticized so that defenses accelerate or self-deprecation is instantaneous. Slow down all responses; suspend judgment until the full message has been heard and considered carefully; and bracket objections until the critic's case has been heard and reviewed. Do not trust your immediate reaction; do not voice your instant explanation; do not utilize any automatic defense.

(2) *Hear the critique as an objection to a part of your personality or self-presentation.* Do not interpret a criticism as a total rejection of the whole of you, but as a potential correction of a part of your personhood. When total language is used, break it down into the smallest reasonable part, the lowest common denominator rather than the larger. Look for specific issues, not general criticisms.

(3) *Accept the confrontation as a comment on your behavior, not an assessment of your worth.* Disconnect self-esteem from the particular exchange that is taking place. Your value as a person is not negotiable on the basis of your interpersonal success at the moment. You are of irreducible worth, whether being respected or rejected, being effective or being stymied.

(4) *Reduce the intensity of the emotions felt* in order to respond intentionally, not react instinctively. When instincts of survival, safety or security direct your thoughts and feelings or help select your words, you are less free to choose how to relate to the other.

(5) *Translate the language that you are hearing from volatile to more neutral,* from inflammatory to informational. As you neutralize the trigger words used by the other, you not only are in a better position to hear more clearly, but you are also less likely to mirror the same feelings that the other is putting on you.

(6) *Reply to the observations that are reported, and not to the conclusions;* to the descriptions of your behavior while ignoring judgments as far as is possible. Go back to the actual observations to learn all you can; do not be caught by the judgments that are offered. Listen for adverbs that report quantity rather than adjectives that label quality.

(7) *Take time—go by your own time needs* and do not let yourself be rushed, pushed, pressured by the other person's pace or impetuosity. Claim your right to reflect, review conflicted feelings and mull it over before replying to criticism.

(8) *Maintain clear boundaries of responsibility.* Define them for yourself clearly, cleanly, sharply and hold to them firmly. The other has the right to report what he/she chooses to give; you have the right to consider it and decide what part to use, how to use it, when you will do so.

(9) *Use positive self-talk in thinking through the criticism.* "I am open to hear your criticism of my behavior; I will take it into consideration with my responsible self. I am willing to hear your critique of choices and actions; I will weigh it as I evaluate whether or not to change. I will take your confrontation seriously. I will see it as significant information but not as the whole set of data that will go into my decision. I am fully responsible for all that I do; I am not to blame.

SCRIPTURE INDEX

SUBJECT INDEX

ENDNOTES

1. John Powell, *Why Am I Afraid to Tell You Who I Am?* (Los Angeles: Argus Communications, 1969).
2. Frank Kimper, "Love and Anger," unpublished manuscript (Claremont, CA: School of Theology, 1971). Used by permission.
3. Harry Stack Sullivan, *The Psychiatric Interview* (New York: W. W. Norton, 1954), pp. 218-219.
4. Ibid., p. 109.
5. Erik Erikson, *Identity and the Life Cycle* (New York: International Universities Press, 1959).
6. Carl R. Rogers and Barry Stevens, *Person to Person: The Problem of Being Human* (New York: Dell Publishing Co., Inc.), pp. 92-94.
7. Friedrich Nietzsche, *The Complete Works of Friedrich Nietzsche,* ed. Oscar Levy (New York: Gordon Press, 1974).
8. Frank W. Kimper, *Meditations for Churchmen in the 70s,* 2nd ed. (Claremont, CA: School of Theology, 1971).
9. Josie Carey and Fred Rogers, "I Like You As You Are," Copyright 1959, Vernon Music Corporation. International copyright secured. All rights reserved. Used by permission of the copyright owner.
10. Hubert Schwartzentruber, *Probe,* James Fairfield, ed. (Scottdale, PA: Herald Press, 1972), pp. 80-81.
11. Thomas Keneally, *Schindler's List* (New York: Simon and Schuster, 1982).
12. David Augsburger, *Dissident Discipleship: A Spirituality of Self-Surrender, Love of God, and Love of Neighbor* (Grand Rapids, MI: Brazos Press, The Baker Publishing Group, 2006).
13. Leo Tolstoy, *The Pathway to Life: Teaching Love and Wisdom* (New York: Cosimo Classics, 2006; Originally published, 1919), p. 40.

ABOUT THE AUTHOR

David Augsburger has taught at Fuller Theological Seminary in Pasadena, California, since 1990. He is currently the professor of pastoral care and counseling at the Fuller School of Theology. David has authored more than 20 books in pastoral counseling, marriage, conflict and human relations, including *Christian Counseling: An Introduction* (with H. Newton Malony, 2007); *Dissident Discipleship: A Spirituality of Self-discovery, Love of God and Love of Neighbor* (2006); *Hate-work: Working Through the Pain and Pleasures of Hate* (2004); *Helping People Forgive* (1997); *Conflict Mediation Across Cultures* (1992); *Pastoral Counseling Across Cultures* (1986); *The Freedom of Forgiveness* (1995); *Sustaining Love* (1989); *Anger, Assertiveness and Pastoral Care* (1985); and the caring series of five books, beginning with the widely published *Caring Enough to Confront* (1980).

Before coming to Fuller, Augsburger taught at seminaries in Chicago, Indiana and Pennsylvania. For more than a decade, he served as radio spokesperson for the Mennonite Churches. His productions won 10 awards for creative radio, television public service and religious broadcasting. He has written feature articles that have appeared in more than 100 different periodicals. As an ordained minister of the Mennonite Church and a diplomat of the American Association of Pastoral Counselors, Augsburger is active in teaching counseling and leading workshops internationally on topics such as pastoral counseling, conflict management in the Church, cross-cultural counseling and theology, cross-cultural conflict and mediation, and forgiveness and reconciliation.